MISSING KEYS

THE STAFF OF LIFE AND ITS SPIRITUAL CONNECTION TO YOUR HEALTH AND HOW TO MANIFEST A MORE POSITIVE LIFE

CelesteLMusick

BALBOA.
PRESS
A DIVISION OF HAY HOUSE

Balboa Press books may be ordered through booksellers or by contacting:

Balboa Press
A Division of Hay House
1663 Liberty Drive
Bloomington, IN 47403
www.balboapress.com
1 (877) 407-4847

Because of the dynamic nature of the Internet, any web addresses or links contained in this book may have changed since publication and may no longer be valid. The views expressed in this work are solely those of the author and do not necessarily reflect the views of the publisher, and the publisher hereby disclaims any responsibility for them.

The author of this book does not dispense medical advice or prescribe the use of any technique as a form of treatment for physical, emotional, or medical problems without the advice of a physician, either directly or indirectly. The intent of the author is only to offer information of a general nature to help you in your quest for emotional and spiritual well-being. In the event you use any of the information in this book for yourself, which is your constitutional right, the author and the publisher assume no responsibility for your actions.

Any people depicted in stock imagery provided by Thinkstock are models, and such images are being used for illustrative purposes only.
Certain stock imagery © Thinkstock.

Print information available on the last page.

ISBN: 978-1-5043-6401-0 (sc)
ISBN: 978-1-5043-6402-7 (e)

Balboa Press rev. date: 10/18/2016

DEDICATION

I dedicate this book to
Carmen C. and Jason Mc.
and their family
without them this would not have
been possible.
To my children and their significant others
for their help, support, love, and patience:
Willie and Laura
Daniel and Heather
Jamie and Clint
Zakery and Sabrie
Kristoffer A.
and to my grandchildren:
Levi, Sidney, Kanada, Randall, and Skyler.
I also want to acknowledge the following people
Randy, Mark, Janice and Paul, Aaliyah for all
their contributions.

INTRODUCTION

I need to tell you there is no quick fix to changing who you are. There is no quick fix to changing who you are. I ask everyone, *"How old are you? How long it it take you to create who your are today?"* There are no overnight fixes. It takes work to heal and to manifest what you want with knowledge and understanding.

This book is what you needed to do before reading the bestselling book that hit the market years ago written on the Law of Attraction. It will explain why most of you are having trouble manifesting what you want in life and how to maintain your health, happiness and more.

It is about how spiritual energy works with and in our bodies and how it gets activated on all our levels of our existence. I will use the Staff of Life to demonstrate this as effectively as I can. The Staff of Life's symbolic meaning refers to our overall health. The Staff of Life not only represents the physical health of a person but it also represent our mental/ emotional and spiritual health as well.

I have been a spiritual healer and teacher for over twenty years and it still leaves me in awe, at how low people's perceptions are today concerning how important spiritual healings are. I worry about everyone's intense insistence on staying who they are and their need to stay in denial. Their assertion of who they really are in this day-in-age is detrimental to their spiritual/soul growth and cleansing.

There are so many people out there who don't know what it takes to eliminate the negative out of their lives. I truly believe they think they have transformed the negative but in reality they have failed. They feel as though they are being positive when they aren't. They can't see themselves, or they do, and they deny it. I believe this is because they lack an understanding of the basic foundational knowledge they need to change. The change is however quite simple. This book should give you the information you need to heal. Plus give you a better understanding of what spiritual/energy is and how it works. It should also help you to boost your spiritual advancement. All it takes is *honesty*.

I based this book on many things. One, is to the family that shunned me because of my spirituality. I am writing about the lessons I have learned from them. I have to thank them for that. If it were not for them I wouldn't be writing this book. They sent me on a journey and on a path that is Divinely connected. What they did to me so many years ago released and freed my soul and spirit from it chains.

Without them I would not be able to help others to heal. They taught me how to release them as a family and get a new family. They showed me there is love in release. Most of us who have done a lot of energetic healings and are on a path to enlightenment know about cleaning spiritually and what I mean by that. They taught me non-attachment. Without them I don't know where I would be today physically, mentally, emotionally, and spiritually/soul.

I said I had many reasons for writing this book. The next reason was to help people to stop suffering. I have truly helped a lot of people. I am writing this book because I want to help many more people get a jump start on their soul's journey. To help them to heal because it is past time! The first step to inner peace and freedom is the healing of your negative emotions. You will see what I mean by this as you read the book. Seriously, the *many reasons* is all the people who need this.

Another reason is because I don't want anyone to go through what I went through. The family has no idea what they have done. But I am putting the information to good use. It is to help others. Someday I will write about that too but for now I will focus on this topic.

There are many more reasons but I am one that uses very few words, as you will find out. For now all you need to do is read the information and understand the content. I believe I wrote it simply enough for the majority of the people. I deliberately kept it as short as I could so you don't lose focus. If you should have any questions however send them to me I will be more than happy to answer them.

I have put together a four point spiritual program for those who want hands-on training and healing. I have put together an interactive prayer to accompany this book for those who are interested. You can find this prayer on my website at: celestelmusick.com.

This book was written to show examples of some of the topics I teach but not all. There is too much information to put it all in one book. It is accumulative in nature and not separate from the information before or after it. The information is daunting and overwhelming to say the least. Just hang in there it will make sense eventually. I am repetitive with the information in this book and this is intentional on my part. You will find similar pieces information though out the book. This is to keep it fresh in your memory and to remind you that all things are connected. The information fits everywhere and not just in one spot. So keep this in mind as you go too. You will need to keep piecing the information together until it makes a whole. It is like a puzzle with each piece needing to fit and connect to the rest of the information in some way. The picture that I am trying to paint for you will begin to develop as you go. This information is to help provide you with stepping stones for those seeking enlightenment and to help boost you a little further and faster on your path or to add to what you already know.

I feel most people have started their journey of enlightenment to increase their vibrations to a higher frequency in the middle of their journey. They have missed crucial beginning concepts to advance them in a knowledgeable and understanding way. I am giving you a primer so to speak to help prevent backsliding from occurring. This information is to build a solid foundation so they can advance a lot quicker in their journey. This will teach them to recognize when they begin a backward spiral and will be able to stop it before they slide too far back. Keep in mind when you do a backward slide you will start all over again.

CONTENTS

CHAPTER 1

DOING YOUR PART

This was very difficult for me to write because of where I am in my understanding of Spirit/energy and my spiritual journey. I have decided to write this book the way I teach the class which is starting with your limited beliefs concerning common aspects that we all possess. Doing it this way begins the process of release of those beliefs to establish a new way of looking at the world from a Universal mind-set. It is my hope the information in this book will advance the ones just beginning their search for enlightenment and those who have already started their journey. I really tried to write using words that connect to a variety of people and beliefs. I may have fallen short on this possibly, but that is okay. I believe what I have written will affect you in such a profound way that you will walk and talk it throughout your life, as well as affect those for whom you touch in your lifetime. To become a person of change.

The information in this book will work for you even though we are all different. We may all vibrate differently. It is only in how we decide to use it that we transform it. My goal is to provide some missing key/s of information that you may still be searching for and to help those who are just beginning their spiritual journey. When you decide to step up to help from a Universal mind set—in essence you are raising your hand to the spirit world and saying, *"Hey! Look at me. I Am ready to do my part, count me in."* You are standing up to be counted and recognized to help with calling in the millennium of peace that all cultures have prophesied about.

We are in the middle of a Spiritual war. The prize is your Soul. Here is your chance to reclaim your Soul and really make a difference. The information contained within these pages will help you to achieve that.

The claiming of your Soul starts with being who you were intended to be. A Spiritual Being that is made of positive energy not a low vibrational being made of negative energy that some religions term 'evil'. Negative energies equals 'evil or bad'. Give up your negative ways and you can reclaim your Divine Soul. I feel today bad/evil is seen as good and good is being seen as 'bad/evil'. I have seen so many 'good' spiritual people being persecuted by those who are negative. These negative people don't see themselves as being negative they seem to *think* they are being positive. This is denial. Not owning your stuff.

Today lies are being seen as okay to do. We need to make a stand. Start standing up for what is right. Being neutral is no longer acceptable. Why? Because you are being asked to make a choice, for lack of better terms, to choose a side that is either positive/good or negative/bad. When you remain neutral you are still exposed to both negative and positive. You can and will be influenced by both. This is not really making a choice so therefore you are not choosing the side of the Divine. The only way to avoid this is to choose where you want to be. You are being asked to stand up. So make a choice!

This information contained in this book is not intended for you to run around and start telling people they have issues. If you are doing this then you have the issue not them. It is to help you to see your own issues and to hopefully open your eyes to what you need to work on. It will help you to accept people for who they are. It will also help you to have acceptance in all things without judgments of any kind. This will be evident to you as we go.

The only way to become positive is to really look at yourself. Not at others. You need to dig down deep and be honest with yourself and what you're doing in all areas. To affect change in the world has to START with you. Once you do this then you will affect others around you. You need to be honest! Most people are not honest with themselves, they sit in denial of who they really are. They refuse to acknowledge their negative speech, behaviors, thoughts, their every aspect that is negative. If someone tells you that you are being negative, maybe, just maybe this is something you need to look at, find and change. Most people won't change it though. They make excuses as to why it isn't negative or they put down the person saying it, so they don't have to change. This is where they mess up.

Picture yourself like an onion. Once you get one layer shed then another one will present itself. No, it isn't easy but you spent your whole life becoming who you have created. In order to affect change it will take some time as well as lots of courage, persistence and the willingness to change on your part. To reach enlightenment you start with you and the information I am giving to you in this book applies to what needs to be done, to start making the changes you need to achieve this.

CHAPTER 2

HEAVEN, BLISS, NIRVANA, RELIGION

Just keep in mind there is more than one way to reach Nirvana, Heaven, Bliss, Grace, or Enlightenment, whatever you want to call enlightenment in your belief system. Those who claim their way is the only way have been lead to believe this through blind faith. This is a control mechanism used by people of power. To get control of you through your belief system. Know there is more than one way to reach enlightenment. There are multiple ways. There is no such thing as "one path." Just as each of us are different on all levels and in every aspect of our being means that some of us need a different way or path than other people follow to achieve Enlightenment. This is not wrong it just means we do and think differently than other people. What works for one does not work for others. So don't judge their path. They are finding their way too, just like you.

Religion:

Try to remember some of the bloodiest wars ever fought throughout history was over religion. Why? When there is ONLY ONE CREATOR! You are fighting against your own Creator! WAKE UP PLEASE! Anytime you hate anything through your belief system, and I don't care who or what it is, then something is wrong.

Those who claim this *"one way to enlightenment"* have chosen through free will to conform and mold their thinking to walk only that one-way path. A negative inflexible path. This blinds them into not accepting other paths that others may choose to follow as their Divine path. These people only think inside the box they were put in. They possess no respect, acceptance, flexibility or tolerance of someone else's beliefs if it conflicts with theirs. This is purely fear based thinking. This tells me they are full of fears. They need to find what they are truly afraid of.

But we can't blame it all on them. They were taught this by those who they *thought* were in power, were *more superior Divinely* then they were and *knew more* than they did. When this happened they took your power. When you gave them your power they got control of you through your belief system.

We could stop wars, violence, achieve tolerance, peace and a lot more if only we would let people believe the way they want to believe. If they are not harming anyone then what difference does it make? I don't see a problem with this. I do see a problem with those who feel their way is the only way and they harm someone for not believing the way they do. This includes physical, mental, and emotional harm. There is no difference. You are not Divine or God like if you choose to harm another. Through lying, rumors, gossiping, abuse, and much much more. How can you be? God is only Good! Your actions have shown you have chosen the side of 'evil/bad'.

I don't know about you but if Creator wanted you dead the Creator wouldn't ask us to do it for Him/Her, that's for sure. Creator would just do it. Creator is All Powerful, remember? Don't use Creator as a weapon to destroy, to kill, harm anything in Creation, or to benefit you in any way at the expense of others. This is a violation of their Free Will which is a Divine Gift from the Creator. If you believe this is what Creator stands for then you have definitely been DECEIVED by those dark forces we term 'evil/bad'!

I have heard people say they did it in the name of their God. Seriously! How did we become blind to the fact that we are tainting what the Creator really stands for. Creator definitely does not symbolize doing anything bad. You only use it as an excuse to do harm in the name of the Creator. Thinking there will be no consequences. Think about it? You're the one doing the harm not them. THERE IS ONLY ONE CREATOR! There is no such thing as "My God" or "Your God" it is "OUR GOD"! Think seriously about what this entails especially if you violate Free Will and interfere with their Divine Plan. You think you can defy the Creator and get by with it, then go ahead. I don't want to be around, especially upon your death.

CHAPTER 3

ACCEPTANCE

I f it were you, wouldn't you want acceptance? Even if you believed
differently than other people? We could have peace if we could just
understand and practice this. Acceptance is also for those of you who
don't believe or don't have a religious or spiritual belief system. Remember,
you can still achieve what you want in life by just leading a good life and
showing it in all aspects of your being.

Leave people alone in their search for enlightenment. It is between
them and the Divine on which path they chose to follow. No one is above
the Creator. No one person has the right to dictate to someone that they
feel are following the wrong path just because it is different from theirs.
You're not the One and Only Creator. The Creator actually puts you on
your path through the Divine Plan that each individual has with the
Creator when they are born. Who are you to decide a path is wrong? Quit
pushing your beliefs off on someone who doesn't want them. That is your
path not theirs and it doesn't mean they are right and your are wrong but
keep in mind it doesn't mean you are right and they are wrong either. It
just means Creator has chosen a different path for them to follow. Quit
interfering with Divine Plan. Be assured ALL beliefs will lead you to
enlightenment just keep in mind no one path is better than any of the
other paths. You have chosen what path you are to follow in this lifetime
through your birth contract. A birth contract is a contract you made with

the Creator before you were born. Let people make their own choices. This allows them to follow their own paths unimpeded.

If you immediately start to discard this thought you may want to stop and consider the statement I gave about giving your power away. You are being controlled through blind faith and it is time to WAKE UP! You are exactly what they want in a person. Start thinking for yourself. Quit being a follower. Become a leader. Trust yourself enough to know, that if you are reading something that is written and it rings true with you, then chances are it is true. Trust what you are feeling. Don't let fear rule you.

CHAPTER 4

WHEN GOD SPEAKS TO YOU

I just love it when someone says to me that, God spoke to them and said it was okay for them to do whatever it was they did. You can't use Creator to do bad and justify what you have done by throwing the Creator into the mix because you feel bad about it. Thinking you are forgiven. Learn to own it and take responsibility for what you have done. When you decide to do anything that is wrong or you decide to interfere with someone's Divine journey then you have taken it upon yourself to override the other person's Divine contract they have with the Creator. You have, in essence challenged the authority of the Creator when you did this. How do you figure this will not come back on you? This is a pretty terrible act to commit against the Creator and toward any other person. Don't you think? Wonder what your repercussions will be? Start taking responsibility for your free will choices and quit using the *"Creator told me I could"* as an excuse to go against Divine Plan just because something doesn't suit or fit within your beliefs! This is similar to throwing a temper tantrum in an evil manipulative way! There is major karma associated with this. You have just violated the Creator and their Divine Plan. The Creator stands for the HARMING OF NONE in every way. What is preventing you from seeing this? Is it the blind faith I spoke of or maybe it is low perceptions? It has to be something? Choose to do what is right this is truly the Divine way! The point is we need to start finding out what it is on an individual basis so we can end it and have peace. Remember Creator WILL NOT tell you to do anything bad or wrong or interfere with someone's Divine will. You chose to do the wrong BECAUSE of YOUR FREE WILL CHOICES that has nothing to do with the Creator. So quit using that as an excuse to justify your behavior or as a reason to do harm to others.

CHAPTER 5

BEFORE THE LAW OF ATTRACTION

This information is focused on, Before The Law of Attraction. This info will be briefly reference later in this book. The subject matter has been gathered from my experiences, through the students and teachings I have done. It is based on the research and knowledge that I have acquired over the years. It is also founded on my understanding of energy and on the experiences that I have had with this energy in my lifetime. I took these experiences and applied the knowledge and understanding I have of it and put it all together. This to show you how energy works within our energetic field, physical body and how it affects our spirit/soul, mind and body.

This is my view of how energy works and how it interacts with all our different levels. What affects you on one level will also affect the other levels of your being in some way. One way to look at this is to envision a rainbow. The colors are separate yet adjoined to the one next to it which relates to the other colors. With each color having its own separate vibrational existence, yet still remaining connected and separate from all the others. Let's imagine each color flowing back and forth exchanging their light and vibrational information with all the other colors. With each color possessing its own unique vibration. This type of interaction creates a cohesive unified whole, working in harmony and balance. Each of these colors touch, flow, and inform the others. This is how our different layers work within our energetic field. We are different yet connected to everyone and everything in Creation. We are light, vibration and information that constantly exchanges spiritual energy and information with each other and with all of Creation.

We know when we look at the rainbow each color appears separate, just remember they all stem from One Source of Light. We too stem from this Source of Light. This One Source of Light which we call the Creator. Remember that each color of the rainbow has its own vibration and has an interaction with the other colors. Like the rainbow we have layers in our energetic makeup that vibrate differently and inform the other layers. It would help your understanding of what I am saying throughout this book if you can see your layers as the colors in a rainbow. We have different vibrations like each color in the rainbow making each of us unique and different. Each of our thoughts, actions, objects/things, behaviors, etc. has its own vibrations. These vibrations are created based on its density, whether it is positive/light or negative/heavy.

Chapter 6

SELF-HELP BOOKS

Everywhere I look today I see self-help books. There are a lot of books on the market written on positive thinking and positive action. They contain information on how you can manifest a better life, health, abundance and more. They are absolutely wonderful! The problem I kept running into is no matter how much I practiced the positive I always had negative issues that kept coming up. These issues would present themselves and I had to deal with them so they wouldn't cancel the effect or block the positive. It felt like I would take ten steps forward and twenty steps backwards. I decided with the help of introspection, meditation, lots of energetic healings and with some information that I had gathered from people, research, and experiences, to try and solve what I consider to be some of the problems I had encountered.

First thing I had to do though was to Wake Up and throw away what I thought made me—me. I cleaned the slate of everything, including my limited beliefs and started all over again. I had to rebuild by foundation on my truths only. But first I had to find them. This book will help you to rebuild your foundation too. But from your truths and not someone else's.

I would also like to try to touch lightly on some issues that I have seen and encountered in the current healing and spiritual enlightenment trends being brought on by the current shift of energies. These new energies that are coming in today are affecting all people. With these new energies comes a whole new set of problems. Especially if you are trying to become more enlightened. A lot of these problems can be avoided however with knowledge and understanding of what is happening.

CHAPTER 7

HEALING

I don't know where to begin here. There are so many different aspects concerning this. Healing starts with you *seeing and owning who you truly are and then changing it.* You will see what I mean as you read this book. Most people can't believe that this is one of the answers they need to ease or eliminate their pain, their dis-ease, their mental, emotional issues and more. It did for me. You need to continue to see your medical field professionals. They are necessary and when you add a spiritual practice to it you can heal.

True healing starts to occur when you begin removing the negative/ heavy energy within your energy field so the energy we call the Light of Creator or positive/light energy can flow freely. Light energy (also known as Divine Creator energy) is the healing energy you need for any and all healing. When you do this, healing starts to occur on all levels of your being. If you want to heal then you must change your negative aspects into positive. You need to really look at yourself. True healing begins in the spiritual/energetic layer. Why? Simple, we can create our reality with the little spark of Divine Light that we all possess that makes us able to create. We hear all the time that we create our lives. This is what I am referring to. This applies to all things including healing. We just need to know how to remove the negative blocks that caused the problems to begin with. This is where alternative spiritual healing methods come in.

We kind of have the idea of what it takes to heal. Most people really get into the healing mode especially after a life altering event. They feel they need to make major positive changes in their lives. They realized they needed to stop being negative and practice being more positive in order to heal themselves. But once the life threatening event is over then they are done with trying to be more positive and they go back to their old selves only to get sick again. I see this happen all the time.

I feel people need to know more about how and what energy is and how it works on a spiritual or energetic level. Knowing this allows you to heal and to help maintain and insure a healthy lifestyle.

What I have written I hope will help with this aspect. You begin the healing and clearing process by looking at who you really are, and by being honest with yourself. It won't work if you not honest. Close your eyes and go inside to the world of spirit. Your spirit. Look at who you really are. Get rid of all your masks. The faces you show to others. The ones you want them to see. Then change it! Wearing mask is deceptive and negative. Be proud of who you are.

CHAPTER 8

DECEPTIONS, EXAGGERATIONS, OMISSIONS, LYING

I am writing this section using the word lying because this is the word used the most by everyone today. I would prefer to use truths and untruths, fact or fiction but lying simplifies things a bit for a better understanding of what I want to convey. Everyone knows what the other words mean but they seem to have a different impact than the word lying does when you use it. This is one of the most important parts in this book for people to understand.

I don't know when it became acceptable in today's world to even think that lying is okay! Not even a little white lie is acceptable! We find it in our belief systems, court systems, governments, in people. It is everywhere. There is no area untouched by this epidemic. What happened to the practice of truthfulness?

There is so much meaning in old sayings. They contain so many keys to enlightenment on what we should do. We have lost the understanding or misinterpreted the meaning somehow. We say it but we don't do it. The one that applies here is, *"a person is only as good as their word"*. I am not sure where that saying came from but I remember my Dad saying that a handshake was as good as your word too. Well back in those days it was.

People lie today so naturally that it has become a second nature to them and when confronted they have a justifiable reason for their lying, or another lie to explain their lie, or just plain denial that they even lied. If you cannot be truthful you won't be able gain acceptance or connection to the Higher Realms. The Creator realm or access to your God Brain/Unconscious.

What's wrong with the truth? Most don't or won't tell the truth because they don't want to take responsibility for their actions, or to suffer the consequences of their actions, or they cover their behavior with a lie to look better in someone else's eyes. Maybe they are playing some sort of role they have created for themselves. For instance, the role of the innocent, the mistreated, the righteous, the justified, whatever the reason we need to release them. They would rather let someone else take the fall for them then to stand up and admit the truth. When did this become an acceptable practice?

I want to explain why being truthful is one of the most important practices in your journey to enlightenment. Keep your promises or your word. Speak the truth. If you say you are going to do something then do it. Of course life happens and if it does do the ethical thing and let others know and explain to them the situation truthfully. In order to create what you want in your life you must not contradict your intent otherwise it will not manifest. If your word is not true and means little to yourself or others manifestation will be delayed or not occur at all until you are able to be truthful with yourself and others. Hence, prayers are so important in this type of situation to help manifest a healing for someone or something of importance in their life. The other reason is it blocks your throat chakra and this chakra is your spiritual connection to your angels, guides, masters, etc. Start speaking truths and this chakra will unblock.

Exaggerations stem from adding information to truths making it a partial truth. It is in reality a deception or lie. Even though it has some truth to its parts. You must be completely truthful in all that you do. If you can't be truthful in everything you do then your Divine connection, healing and anything you may want to create in your life will not take place.

Omissions are still deceptive. Telling someone the truth and leaving parts of it out is still deceitful. You must be upfront and truthful at all times with all the information no matter what it is. No one says you have to tell everything you know. But if you start be prepared to tell all the truth not just parts of it.

If someone ask you something and you don't want to answer then you tell them that you don't want to answer. You have free will which gives you that right. Maybe you're not answering because it would affect someone else. You are not obligated to tell them why. There are many scenarios you can come up with for this section and each one should be evaluated as separately. You should never assume that because one incident is similar in facts that it is the same for everyone. Categorize them as either fact or fiction, truth or untruths.

I was taught in college that human beings would complete a story if it was missing a part, for example a beginning or ending. That this was a natural human aspect. Please don't do this. Just say, *"That is all I know about it."* Don't exaggerate or elaborate any fact/s in a story this is also a deception. Here is where I want to relay an example to give you an idea of what I am talking about that pertains to this section.

There were ten people who witnessed the same accident involving a car crash. They all saw the same accident as it was occurring. Some from the same angle, others from different vantage points with everyone having different perceptions of what happened. When questioned by the officer he found out that all ten stories were different with just a few elements remaining the same. For example, they all knew there was an accident that involved two cars. From there the story changes per person.

Were they lying or telling the truth? None of them were wrong. They witnessed it from their level of understanding or perception and from their vantage point. This is their truth. Now this is where it gets catchy. Where do we go with our understanding of this? When in essence with this example they were all being truthful. None of them were lying. I usually accept it for what it is. What else can you do? We need to start accepting it for what it is without comments or judgments of any kind.

A few of those ten people. Those who didn't see the whole incident and only saw the ending made-up the first part. Don't do this. Just say, *"I don't know"*. Do not make up any fact/s because you are missing them to complete a story. This is a lie and an exaggeration. I know it is human nature to complete the story but it is not the truth and it will create energy blocks in your system.

Then you have people you just blatantly lie and they know it. When you confront them some will tell you up front that they are lying. This is rare but it does happen. Then we have those who deny they ever lie and will not admit the truth even if you stood them on their head. This happens the majority of the time.

We also have those who mix truth and lies. These people are the most dangerous of liars. I have seen these types of people fool court systems, law enforcement, organizations, anyone and everyone actually. They mix just enough truth with the lies that they can and do fool everyone to achieve what they want at the expense of others. Accomplished liars are very manipulative and clever. I know I have a family full of them. They can make you believe them over someone who is being truthful. It is an art form that is becoming common place. These people get upset when they actually get caught lying. Or they act like nothing happened. What!? For those who are truthful beware of these types of people. Be cautious of confronting this type of person because they are very vengeful and wrathful people. They will do and stop at nothing to achieve their destruction of you. They never forgive even if they are wrong. Because in their minds they are the victim. Isolate and eliminate these people if you can out of your life. They are toxic and extremely dangerous. If you can't eliminate them out of your life I suggest you distance yourself. Take everything they say with a grain of salt. These are very *selfish self-centered* people with their own agenda and they exhibit little or no compassion.

I also want you to keep in mind that in all the areas that I mentioned before, like the court systems etc., can and are fooled by these types of people, these too are occupied and ran by very deceitful individuals. If you develop a higher level of perception you can detect these people quite easily.

On the flip side if you don't really want to hear the truth then please don't ask the question/s. Most people will not out of courtesy and respect mention certain things. There are some people who get mad at you for telling them the truth. I believe this is where people do lie just to save someone's feelings. Lying is never good to do even to save someone's feelings. Tell them the truth but do it gently. So if you are in doubt about hearing the answer, keep the question to yourself. This will keep you from getting upset at them when technically it isn't their fault they spoke the truth in the first place because you asked them. So why are you upset? Start taking responsibility for your actions and quit placing blame. Truthfully it is time for the lying, corruption and ALL negative behaviors to stop.

CHAPTER 9

WHAT IS RIGHT AND WRONG?

Seems funny I have to write on this topic because we believe people know the difference. I found out most don't or they don't understand the difference. Some blatantly just don't care. So why is it important? See if you can figure it out as you read this book.

Right or wrong also creates a vibrational energy. EVERYTHING creates a vibrational energy and it can be either negative or positive in nature. Believe it or not everything is energy you will see what I mean by this as we go. Everything that we do creates energetic loops that will come back to you or to those who are connected to you genetically. This refers to Karma and the energetic/spiritual return of all things.

Everyone has their own interpretation of what is considered right or wrong. It is based individually on the actions associated with an event or situation and the person's own perception of right or wrong. Perceptions vary depending upon the person's individual teachings they had throughout life and from their upbringing. They see nothing 'wrong' with what they are doing. It is natural for them because it is based on their experiences, their raising. Their perceptions come from what they are accustomed to, or the people they are surrounding themselves with. They have developed perceptions that come from how they view the world. They have incorporated these based on how they tried to understand the world around them. So we shouldn't judge or condemn anyone because our precept is different from someone else's perceptions.

Some judgments seen today come from the differences between high level perceptions, stemming from a Universal Mind and low level perceptions coming from a selfish self-centered mind. These lower perceptions come from our limited beliefs which are nothing more than opinions. They are based on how we view life supported by events in our upbringing, our ego and more. Sometimes people get stuck here and can't move past this low vibrational perception. You can't tell these people anything because it comes from a selfish self-centered perspective. You know who they are. They are the people who are always right, they know it all, they never hear you, nor do they listen, they will do it their way, etc… Don't mess with them you can't convince them of anything. It is best just to walk away from these types of people.

All spiritual traditions, all cultures, the different societies speak about what is right and wrong. We seem to want to decide what is right and wrong based on loosely defined definitions and opinions. The definition to decide the differences between right and wrong should be based on these three questions. Does this interfere with someone else's Divine Journey? Does it interfere with their Free Will? Does it harm someone, including yourself, mentally/emotionally, physically, or spiritually? These three questions should definitely be asked then go from there. It wouldn't hurt to ask more questions than these, if at all possible. Like I said it depends on the situation or action associated with it and each incident should be viewed as separate and not judged one way or the other on what you consider, to be right or wrong. If you answered yes to any of these then it is negative/wrong to do. It goes against your Universal Mind, your Unconscious Divine connection.

When I was in one of my college psychology classes I remembered a story my professor told at the time that made me really think of what is right and wrong so I will use it as an example here. I don't know where the story originated but I will relay it nonetheless:

There lived a husband and wife who were happily married for many years but very poor. The wife went to the doctors one day because she fell ill and couldn't overcome the illness. The doctor told her she was going to die the next day if she could not get this one type of medicine. The husband took the prescription to all the pharmacies in town and asked for the medicine for his wife explaining he had no money and without the medicine his wife would die. All the pharmacies refused to give him the prescription to save his wife. So that night he broke into a pharmacy and took the medicine.

Based on your concept of what humane is and according to our laws today what do you think should happen to him? Was he right or was he wrong? What would you have done if it was your loved one? We have to remember that the laws we have today are man-made. Man-made laws are laws created from the conscious side of our brain which is connected to our physical reality and does not stem from the Divine side of ourselves. Being humane is a Divine way to be? So the question is, do we follow Divine Laws or follow what maybe wrong or right based on man-made perceptual laws? Remember that perceptions are individual, concerning right and wrong. You can have a perception based from a selfish self-centered perspective or one that comes from a Universal perspective. Being selfish or being Universal determines which side of the brain you exist most in or are operating from. How did you answer the questions? From a physical perception or from a spiritual perception? There is only two ways to view this...from a Universal Divine Mind or through a mind that is selfish and self-centered. One is the positive and one is the negative.

Another example on a mass scale of right and wrong is the prison systems and all the other organizations that go against Universal Laws. This system and all others that are in existence today need to begin taking the concept of what's right and wrong into consideration in relation to violation of Free Will and other Universal Laws. This system alone is creating a lot karma for themselves, their children and for all future generations to clear. We will have trouble attaining peace if this continues. We will be too busy trying to clear up our families past karma to bring in the peace we so deserve.

We need to be very careful of interference with someone's individual Divine Journey and with the interference of their Free Will, which are gifts from the Creator. These systems are playing with fire when they disregard Divine Laws. Not saying that there shouldn't be some sort of reciprocity due to those who are truly guilty. I am speaking of the innocent people being falsely accused and convicted today because of the current system's operations and rules. The whole prison system needs to be made over. I am sure there are much better solutions than the ones we currently have in place. There are very intelligent people out there who think outside the box who can come up with a better solution to replace our current system.

Today we have prison systems that are set up as privately owned corporations. They make money imprisoning people. They need a constant supply of their product (*people*) and where do you think they are getting them? They need to keep the product (*people*) moving because the more (*people*) they get, the more money they make. Even if someone is wrongly accused. This is how they make money. I just pray the next one convicted isn't a loved one of yours or a relative you love dearly that has been falsely accused and convicted of something they didn't do.

This is one area that we need drastic changes in. I believe that someone will step forward in the future and create a system that focuses on fair humane practices. We need to speak up before it is too late and make the changes so our children's children can inherit a world of peace. Greed has consumed the world and our concept of what is right and wrong is being tainted. What happened to compassion? What happened to our humanity? Wake up please, our world needs it, our children and our children's children need it!

CHAPTER 10

WHAT IS NEGATIVE ENERGY
AND POSITIVE ENERGY?

There is much confusion on what positive and negative is and on what their meanings are. This is not just confined to speech. It is everything about you. It is in every action that you do physically, mentally/emotionally, and spiritually. Meaning negative or positive is found in your thoughts, actions, behaviors, speech and much more. These two polarities are found in all things. We tend to categorize them as being either good or bad. Problem here is people do not see themselves as negative in anything that they do. They have been blinded. Then they try to justify their negative actions, whatever it maybe and claim it is positive. Oh, come on. We all see this. Why can't you? Own it, so you can heal and help make the changes we need in the world.

This makes it very difficult to be spiritual in a world where there is confusion on what these two energies are. I understand people believe they are being positive. But, in reality they're not. If only they would stop long enough to listen to what they are saying. Try to be aware enough of what they're doing. We could change things. Maybe if they would just be honest with themselves, they would be able to see how truly negative they really are. Maybe they don't care. Maybe the development of compassion and the ability to see someone's life from the other person's perspective, would stop the negativity. Like the old saying goes: *"walk a mile in someone else's shoes."* You must be able to FEEL and walk in those shoes before you would realize you're not being positive at all. You're being judgmental. Which is negative. Can't you see this? This is one of the things that leads me to believe that people are confused on what the difference is between the two energies or they are just totally oblivious to what they are doing and saying. Maybe they are aware but just like the drama. They justify their behaviors through their belief systems. Convincing themselves they are forgiven and this allows them to continue to abuse others. Because God forgives all. Yes this is true but you still have that life review that most call Judgment Day to deal with. Trust me you will experience retribution for all you have done.

People who feel they are being positive don't seem to know how they affect someone but are sure to take up arms when it happens to them. They start screaming and complaining about how badly they have been treated. How they were abused. Seriously? They seem to think it is okay for them to do it to someone else but have Mercy if it was done to them. It is time to lay down the swords and think of what you are doing to yourself and others!

People who look from the outside in will quickly see who someone is before they do. But when it is brought to the other person's attention they get angry and defensive toward the person trying to help. These people refuse to accept what they are being told. They use excuses to not see it in themselves because this would require change, honesty, courage and effort from them in order to shift the energy. In their eyes they couldn't be like that.

No one wants to admit to possessing bad habits, behaviors, thoughts, or any negative traits for that matter. This includes me. In reality I can't blame you but if you want to heal you have to truly look at yourself. Keep in mind this is hard for anyone to do! The problem is most people do not see and accept the negatives or shadows within themselves. They have trouble facing the fact that they can be like that. When you are in denial of it then you don't make the changes necessary to make a difference within your health and life. In their eyes the problem is with the other person. They are happy with who they have created and the ego convinces them that it is everyone else who has the problem, not them.

If you want to change then you need to start listening to those who are on the outside looking in. When they tell you that you are acting or speaking negatively instead of ignoring the other person who is trying to help you to see what you are doing. Listen to them. Stop and pause for a moment and take a good look at who you are. Go inside and ask yourself, *"Am I really like that?"* I believe you will see it if are honest with yourself. Just remember these people aren't trying to make you mad they are wanting to help you. Most people tend to get angry, defensive or try to condemn the other person for it. Stop and really look and you just might see what they are talking about. They are just trying to help you, give you a message. So don't ignore, introspect and be honest and chances are you will see it. But only if you are painfully truthful and honest. Then you can make the change/s you need.

Negative energy is heavy dense energy that comes from our 'bad' thoughts, behaviors, actions, violence, rage, speech, rumors, gossiping, lying, cheating, stealing, etc. This includes all our negative emotional reactions to situations that make us feel 'bad' or make us angry and much more. This energy creates emotional blocks within our energy field which stops the flow of healing/positive Divine energy that is needed to keep us healthy spiritually, physically, mentally and emotionally. These blocks throw you out of balance and create dis-eases within you. You need to be in balance to stay healthy on all levels. Eliminate the negative including the emotion connected to all negative events and situations from your life. You will find yourself healthier, happier, and feel more at peace than ever before in your whole life. As you start doing this you will eliminate a lot, if not all, of your negative baggage.

Positive energy is Divine/Creator energy that stems from practicing things like forgiveness, unconditional love, compassion, non-judgment, truthfulness, it is the expression of all things good. The flow of this energy helps remove blocks created by negative emotional energies. This type of energy provides you the healing energy you need to stay healthy on all levels of your being. It is the opposite of negative energy and it is the most powerful.

This just shows you there is only One Source of energy and that energy can be used for both good and bad. There is no discrimination concerning this because it is directed energy. This is the same energy that we use to help or heal others and in reverse it can be used to harm others as well. People harm people all the time without knowing it. It is time for this type of behavior to end.

You harm by directing your negative emotional energy at someone with the intent to harm them spiritually, mentally/emotionally and physically. Like your thoughts, in rumors and gossiping, and much more. This negative directed energy will come back to you. Eventually hurting you worse. Remember all energy returns to its source but with ten times the force. Keep this in mind. To stop this, all we need to do is try to get enough of an understanding of how energy works and what it really is to transform all negative actions into more positive actions.

This will probably be one of the first books ever written that focuses on your negative side and how to balance it with your positive side. When you work on the negative aspects you will no longer be reactive in a negative way or reactive in negative situations either. When you do this inner peace starts to take you over. It is wonderful.

I was no different than anyone else. I also believed I was a good person. Then I realized that I wasn't. I was shocked to discover I wasn't very good at all. Every student I have taught to date are shocked to realize this too. So many times we sit in denial and can't see beyond our own self-centered self. We have convinced ourselves we are a certain way and we are not at all like what we think we are.

Today everybody refuses to look at their negative aspects. They either deny or ignore them. Some claim it is fashionable to do certain behaviors. An example of this, such as lying. They make statements like, *"Everyone is doing it. So it is okay."* For one it makes you a follower and we don't need more followers. We have enough of them already. You are allowing others to think for you when you follow. You could be using this statement to give you a reason to lie. It doesn't matter what it is or why you are lying. The bottom line is, it is not a Divine action. It is negative/bad/evil to do. Being negative is not Divine.

Lying is a negative/bad/evil, whatever you want to call it action. We are to do Divine actions. To do anything that is not positive is harmful to you, your health, happiness, your spiritual growth and more. It will affect everything about you including your death.

You will have lots of problems with trying to be spiritual if you choose to ignore the negative *(because it needs healing first)* and only work on the positive. You need to learn balance to advance your spiritual growth. You must own your other selves. Until you begin to own and heal ALL of your other *(shadow)* selves, the ones we hide in our closets. You will have trouble staying and being in balance and harmony. We don't want them coming up in the future to drag us back to start all over again while we are trying to advance our spiritual growth and connection. So let's heal them instead. I do a program that has had lots of success in doing just this. For it to work it will take effort, honesty, and courage to look at yourself and who you really are. You must also have the courage and the willingness to see what others see in you. Then you can affect change within you and around you.

One of the main reasons it is so hard to get into balance is because nobody deals with their negative aspects or selves. They ignore them, deny them and try to hide from them like they don't exist. These aspects are part of you. Your negative energy is what is creating your issues so why are we ignoring this? It takes healing these to get everything you ever wanted in life. So in order to create a lasting more positive you in this life you must deal with the negatives that you have and heal those first. This allows you to make room to let the positive changes in. When you begin to do this the positive becomes more prominent in everything that you do. You will notice increases in the positive things happening to you. Your thoughts will become more positive. You will begin to feel more Blessed when you start balancing the energies within the spirit/soul, mind and body.

Chapter 11

PROGRAM FOR HEALING

Y ou need to educate yourself and see why it is important to bring the negative and the positive into balance. Most people know how the do the positive side of this. Where they fail is—not healing, balancing and owning their negative aspects. This includes those negative aspects we bury inside ourselves. Burying them will not work. Because they could be dug up at any time. If you have not dealt with the negative aspects of your being on the physical, mental, emotional, and spiritual/soul level then you haven't healed them. They will always keep coming up and interfering with your spiritual advancement. They will interfere in your life preventing you from manifesting what you want in life. If you have suppressed them, it will only come out in the future to taunt you. If you are reactive in any way then the issue still exist within your energetic field.

What are the other selves I spoke about earlier? Again a reminder, they are your angry self, violent self, judgmental self, vengeful self, these and more. They are connected to our triggers, our thoughts, our beliefs, and every aspect of us. They are our emotional responses that live within us that we haven't healed yet or they are connected to reactions that ego has created to defend who you think you are. They are also the negative things that you possess that you don't want others to see in you. Unless you begin to own and heal these you will not achieve your spiritual Oneness with Creator. As I progress throughout this book with the information you will see what I am speaking of.

You cannot get rid of these aspects of yourself, both the positive or the negative aspects. You cannot hide them. You cannot deny them. They are part of you. To do so will leave you feeling empty and wholeness will not be achieved or felt. You will carry a void within you. You must incorporate and own all of your selves in order to be Whole. You must face them and heal them. Replace them by seeing the positive in everything that is negative. It is the only way to achieve Oneness with the Creator. Learn to control the negative emotions and instead of letting your emotions control you. You do this by knowledge, understanding, and healing these within you. When you heal these, you no longer have *'triggers'* or are reactive in stressful situations.

There is a way to heal these negative aspects effectively. Through knowledge and understanding. By finding a program from someone who understands this information and knows how to help you remove these unwanted energies. By doing a little homework on your part you can achieve what I am talking about. These types of programs help you to override these energies and remove them spiritually/energetically. Once this is done it will affect all your other layers, like your physical, mental and emotional levels. Remember the rainbow example?

I have help so many people to finally achieve inner peace. To know the difference between what is positive and what is negative energetically. It is not easy and there are no guarantees. Because it is all up to you and not me whether it works or not. This depends solely upon you. If you are ready to heal and let loose of those emotions causing your problems then it will happen. But, not until you are ready. If you are not ready, the program you chose and the information you acquired through it will always be available to you. So in the future when you get ready to release hopefully you can do this without any help from someone else.

CHAPTER 12

WE ARE BIOLOGICAL BEINGS

I took a few psychology classes while I was attending college and I remembered my college professor making a statement that has stayed with me to this day. He said, *"We are biological beings and we were made never to be sick. So that being said, why do we get sick?"* That statement intrigued me enough to remember it for years. I couldn't answer that at the time but I sure would love to write a paper on that for him now. Maybe this book will suffice. Perhaps he will pick this book up and read it and realize he was the one who gave me the inspiration to find the answer to this question. Even if it was through an event that almost killed me.

I answered this question by going through this life event to heal. I never forgot what he said that day. I know now that remembering that so clearly meant that I would use the information in the future somewhere on my life's path. Possibly for writing this to help expand knowledge on the subject. Maybe to help others to heal. I do know I was meant to remember that question for a reason. That it was part of my life's journey.

The answer to this question is found within the negative energetic parts of ourselves and through others directing negative energies at us. Bottom line we are sick because we are not being who we truly are meant to be. Spiritual beings. Not negative evil beings. Positive spiritual beings. Thanks Julian for that question so many years ago.

CHAPTER 13

RAISING YOUR VIBRATIONS AND STAGNATION

E nergy is always changing, shifting and moving. We are made of
energy. Nothing is constant and unchanging. If we don't change
we can become stagnant. I don't mean change in just the physical
aspects of ourselves and our lives. I also mean, in our conscious and
unconscious way of thinking and being. Changes need to occur on all our
levels so we can grow and stay healthy.

Your different layers need to be put back into balance and harmony so
they can work together efficiently and harmoniously like they were created
to do, eliminating dis-ease within us. Saying that is easy but doing it and
understanding it is harder. You must walk your talk in a positive way or
in other words practice what you preach in everything that you do if you
want to attain balance and harmony. Achieving this will allow you to walk
in Grace once more.

When we get blockages in our energetic field, this stops or slows
down the flow of healing energy needed to keep us healthy on all levels.
Negative energy throws us out of balance and will manifest in many
different negative ways in our life. Blockages occur when we take on
negative energies from others or from accepting the negative energies we
do to ourselves with our thoughts, actions, behaviors and emotions. We
need to raise our vibrations to eliminate these types of blockages within

our energetic field. We raise our vibrations by being positive plus we need to control and not do the negative.

The problem is how do we do that? How can we affect all our levels at one time? Believe it or not we do it all the time. We just don't know we are doing it.

One way to start raising your vibrations is through awareness. Catching the negatives and replacing it with being positive in every action, thought, speech, in all your behaviors, reflecting this from within. Letting the positive flow outward affecting your environment, the people who you surround yourself with and more. Just to name a few.

I gave you a few ways to start turning the negatives around earlier. Like the sections on lying, judgment, right and wrong, etc. This is just a start. Were you paying attention? Start with the small things like these and work yourself up to bigger and more prominent things to heal.

A few simple things you could do to help raise your vibrations:

1. Get Knowledge! Heal! Don't let it in or back in through your emotions.
2. Use Karmic *(aka Mind your Own Business)* Scale!

To raise your vibrations you need to understand what that means. I use two examples in class where I demonstrate what is high and low in vibration and how we can raise our vibrations.

Our energetic field surrounding us is filled with love when we are born. But as we grow and we experience disappointments, traumas, emotional upsets, mental anguish, depression, and others. These negative expressions will take away the love and replace the love we once had with those aspects. We keep holding onto the emotion contained within the event itself. Let it go. This lowers our vibration over time especially when we hang onto the past or the emotional scarring associated with the event/s. We take in these low vibrations and when we bring them into our energetic field we actually decrease the higher vibration of the love (Divine love) that we were gifted with. This is done through the choices we make. With our thoughts. With our emotions. Our actions. We ALLOWED them in. This is known as FREE WILL. They will make you sick! Let them go. Find love and forgiveness in them and start practicing love and forgiveness daily for the rest of your life.

The first thing to do is not let them in. How do we stop this? We can however choose not to allow them in, but many people lack the basic understanding of how this is done. This usually has an emotional connection. To choose not to— means releasing the emotion of that heavy dense negative energy creating the problem. We want to hang onto the emotion/s. We don't want to release that aspect of ourselves that ego has created through our emotions. I will try to explain this, as well as include a few other keys you may be missing that could help you while you are on your spiritual journey.

Classes like what I teach will help you too. But I don't think anyone teaches how the Staff of Life works, except for me. There is nothing on the internet concerning this way of viewing it. I found bits and pieces but none of them are put together to try and create a cohesive whole to show how the physical, mental/emotional, and spiritual/energetic aspects of ourselves work together and not as separate pieces of ourselves. The Staff of Life shows us how to create complete health on all levels by showing us that all areas of our health are interconnected. That what impacts one layer affects the others.

The second is an invisible scale that I give to my students so they can increase their vibrations as well as relieve any karmic debts they may have incurred. I teach them to use it to try to keep any karma created in this lifetime and past lifetimes from manifesting. This scale will also cut down on the amount of negative energy you take on as you live your life. The following is a description of this scale. I call it a Karmic Scale but it is known to my students as *'Mind your own Business Scale (M.O.B.S.)'.*

This scale is numbered from zero to ten with ten being most important in your life and of course you know what zero means. It is not on your scale. This scale has your name on it but there can be many of them with a lot of different titles to represent all the areas of your life. For example your scale may have a lot of different names like: job, relationships, children, friends, family, etc. The title for your scale comes from all the different aspects of your life and on what is currently taking place in your life.

This scale is also useful to stop the drama, rumors and gossiping that most people seem to thrive on today. Using this scale will help clear out blocks created by negative energy. It will keep you from creating more negative energy in your auric field as well as help you bring more positive energies into your life. In the following examples I hope to give you a few ideas of how to use your scale on a daily basis.

1. If you have children under the 'legal age' limit where would they fall on your scale? Hopefully it will be ten, being the most important. Here is the catch. You are to provide *guidance* for their journey in this lifetime. So many parents want to control, dictate, and rule instead of guide. They are your children only in this lifetime. They belong to our Spiritual Mother and Father. So please take excellent care of them. They are our future, our children's future. What if they are over the legal age limit? Where would they fall on your scale? They don't. They are a zero. They have their own Divine path to follow. It is time for you to let them lead their own lives without interference. They must make their own mistakes. The more you try to buffer their fall the more difficult their lessons will be. Let them go if you truly love them! Their lessons will be much easier on them if they are allowed to make their own mistakes. If you keep them from their lessons the lessons will become harder and harder as they progress through life. It can even manifest to the point of immense pain or even trauma for them and so much more. If you love your children—as I suspect you do, then let them fall. Stop trying to buffer their falls. They have to fulfill their birth contracts. This is a contract made between the Creator and them before they were born in this lifetime. You are to guide only. Hopefully they will choose correctly when the time comes but until then we have to let them go. When they are of legal age and they request guidance you can give them advice but they must request it. Other than that there should be no interference. It should be their choice only. It doesn't mean you won't love them anymore it just means you love them more.

2. Let us talk about your partner or spouse. Where would they fall on your scale? They don't. They also fall at zero. The only time they would fall on your scale with importance is when a decision needs to be made that involves you or would affect something in both

your lives. Remember the name on the scale has your name on it not theirs, they have their own scale with their name on it. They too have their own Divine Journey to complete in this lifetime. You are just sharing in part of their journey.

3. What about your job and co-workers? Of course your job is high up on the scale. Your co-workers however are not on your scale at all unless it involves your job duties or job performance. Otherwise they are zero. This also helps stop drama, rumors and gossiping in the workplace. The reason this stops is because your co-workers are not on your scale at all. What if they don't use the scale? If you are the only one using the scale it will only work to improve your work environment. Everyone should practice using this scale because it would stop a lot of stress as well as negative energy in our lives and create a peaceful environment in which to live and work.

You can use this scale regularly throughout your life so you can achieve peace and happiness. Just remember if it doesn't fall on your scale then it is *none of your business*. This scale is just simply making it so you *mind your own business* and *everyone else mind's theirs*. When you practice this regularly you stop judgments, rumors, gossiping of all things and people. It teaches you to accept people for who they are and situations as something that is for them to learn, witness, or experience as they travel on their own journey. We each have our own Divine journeys to complete, keep this in mind.

These are by far NOT the only way/s to raise your vibrations. There are numerous ways to achieve control of the lower vibrations—those negative energies we so fondly display and then claim to be positive. You can just be positive and you will achieve the control of the negative aspects of yourself.

CHAPTER 14

LIKE ENERGY ATTRACTS
LIKE ENERGY

So as we go through life these low-level negative energies that we take on will attract more negative energies. Like energy attracts like energy. If you put energy vibrations on a scale of one to ten with ten being the most important what would be placed at ten? It would be Unconditional Love. If you had to choose what was zero—what would it be? It would be hate. The lowest of all vibrations.

We are born of Light and Love and as we go through life we take the negative aspects on through our negative experiences, thoughts, and more. We bring them into our field and incorporate them through our emotions displacing the higher vibrations of Light and Love putting them somewhere out in the ether. If we don't deal with the 'hate', let's say, we will be consumed with hate eventually. *Like energy attracts like energy, remember?* This works with all our attributes.

Mom and Dad use to say this when I was younger, *"birds of a feather flock together"*, a version of a quote by William Turner. This saying is talking about this like energy. Maybe the other saying that applies here that you may have heard is, *"you are who you hang with"*. So be careful who you choose to be around. When you start taking on this type of energy a buildup occurs in your energetic field it acts like a magnet that keeps drawing to you what you think and feel. This starts the building up and the creating of negative blocks in your energetic field. Like dominoes it will eventually create dis-ease within your different energetic layers, the mental, physical, spiritual, and emotional layers. It will bring in, just to name a few—depression, anxieties, cancers, streaks of bad luck and much more. Remember it displaces your Light and Love that is needed for health, happiness, healing, all positive energies you need to manifest what you want. Right now you are only manifesting the negative because you are out of balance. More negative is going on in your lives than positive. Hence, out of balance.

CHAPTER 15

THERE IS ONLY ONE SOURCE OF ENERGY

There is only One Source of energy that created everything. This energy operates and is in everything in existence. It possesses different densities, forms, information and vibrations. Everything is energy. This is what we have been taught throughout our life. This is backed up with what we learned in science classes.

We also have been told by our religious institutions that everything we see is created by the Creator and it is made of Divine energy. Everything is made of Divine Light, vibration, and information. It is Living Energy. This creative force is nothing but pure Divine refined energy that we gave a human form to in order to connect to this Divine essence. Whether you believe in a Divine Source of energy or not the fact remains and is backed up with scientific theory that everything is made of energy. There is only one ENERGY and we call this ENERGY Creator. It is the same ENERGY that science speaks of, studies, and theorizes about. The separation of Church, State and Science was deliberate concerning this part. It kept people from realizing this.

This One Source of energy is called by many different names, for example, Great Spirit, God, Goddess and others. I will use words like Energy, Spirit, Creator, Source of all things, God, Goddess, Christ,

Buddha interchangeably at times to stress a point using names that most people are familiar with because they are one in the same.

It doesn't matter what you call this energy. Everyone worships this One Source. There is ONLY ONE! It really doesn't make sense to me when I see anything written that states they have the one true God or even insinuates there is more than one source of creative energy or that *their* 'God' is better than someone else. Seriously! There is only ONE and we all worship the same One. We just have different names for this One Source based on an individual's religious or spiritual beliefs and their geographic location.

How did we get so many different names? All cultures over time have developed ways to connect to this Divine essence. Each area and culture would give this One Source a name and human image in order to connect. To try to understand and define what they viewed as the Creator. One way was to personify the energy aspect of the Creator they needed to connect to. Personify means to put into human form the aspect they wanted to bring in. The aspect they wanted to relate to was personalized by giving the form a name as well as the human image. Let us use love as an example. This is how Venus came to be— she represents the love aspect of the Creator.

Just like the Creator we all possess the same aspects. I will only use a few but keep in mind there are thousands of different attributes. We have thousands of different aspects that make up our attitudes, personalities, and anything else that makes us who we are.

Each culture had their own name/s to describe Creator and the many different characteristics of the Creator. Keep in mind that the Creator consist of male and female energies. This energy is known as Yin and Yang in eastern philosophies. So each attribute will have either be a male or a female name or both.

See the examples below:

Love: Venus, Aphrodite etc.
War: Morrigan, Anat, Ares, Athena, Jehovah etc.
Hunting: Apollo, Mabon, Artemis etc.
Healing: Apollo, Asklepios, Borvo, Gula, Hala etc.

In the above example I showed a few of these aspects. The point is it doesn't matter what name you use, they all describe and belong to the One Source of Energy we call Creator of all things. So when you condemn someone else's belief or blast the name they use for Creator just remember you are disrespecting and blasting the Creator in your belief too because THERE IS ONLY ONE.

CHAPTER 16

RELIGION VS SPIRITUALITY

There is a huge difference between the major Religions of today and Spirituality. Religion is based upon someone else's experience with the Divine. You are FOLLOWING their truths, visions, and personal experiences. That Creator is outside of you. When you do this it is very rare you will find and have your own Divine encounters and experiences. It teaches you to look outside yourself to make changes in your life or find the answers you are looking for.

Spirituality is finding your own individual connection and experience with the Divine. It is finding inside yourself your Divine Nature. That changes must occur internally before they can be reflected outward.

This is the hardest of paths to follow because you are in charge of saving your soul and no one else. *"Seek and ye shall find,"* as the old saying goes. You need to seek for yourself your own Divine connection. Quit following someone else truths. Build your own truths. Open the doorways into other beliefs with an open mind. It is hard telling where you may find the answers or that Divine connection you are searching for.

Because each of us is different (like I wrote earlier) know that what works for one may or may not work for you or someone else. Actually how can it? We don't always like the same things or do the same things. Do we?

Some of the hardest *limited beliefs* to overcome by some in my class are those based on blind faith and fear that appear in some religious practices. These beliefs come from those systems who tell you not to question and you are to accept it as the truth even though you see it as a lie. A lie is a lie there is no way around this. Wake up! They have convince you through blind faith to accept these lies as truths. Guess what? A lot of you have. These institutions want followers and not people who can think for themselves. They want full control of what you should think, act, do and feel. Beware to those you create conflict by questioning these discrepancies. These institutions begin screaming heresy, blasphemy, the you are going to burn in Hell routine. They use fear to keep you where you are so you won't go anywhere else and you learn to not question their authority. They need you. They need your money. Religion is based on man-made beliefs. This means the words written in Holy Books were not written by God but by man. Which is on the side of our conscious physical human reality. Spirituality on the other hand stems from our God brain, the unconscious side of our brain.

When you begin to think for yourself and start to step outside the box that belief systems keep you in and you start to question things. Just remember the institutions don't want you to question. When you do they start to instill fear in you. These people make you feel as if they are religiously superior to you. Not so, you are equal to those who are standing at the pulpit or those whom you believe have a leg up on you when it comes to being spiritual. The problem is you are lead to believe you have to rely on them to give you, your connection to the Creator. They can't do this. If they could you wouldn't need them. You need to wake up to the fact you are equal to them spiritually and your connection to Creator must be done by you and only you. No one else can do this but you.

We are all children of the Creator, just keep this in mind. They don't want you knowing this so you are taught to believe you need "saving," and if you question you will be condemned to a fate of misery. These are fear based beliefs. This leaves you feeling fearful and vulnerable to some of the negative teachings that are found in belief systems. You then allow fear to rule you. With fear ruling, you go no further in thought and in your search for the Divine. This can leave you feeling more lost than ever before. These types of teachings are based on greed, control, and submission to the institution who is placing that fear there. It is okay to question and follow your own path. When you do begin to find Grace, Bliss, Blessings, Nirvana and Heaven within your life and much more. Peace will fill your life and that void will no longer be inside you. I know. This is how I found it.

CHAPTER 17

RESTRICTING BELIEFS, OPINIONS, TRUTHS

What I am going to discuss may not fit into your belief system yet. That is okay. All I ask is that you don't discard it. Like I tell my students, *"Don't throw it away put it up on a shelf for later reference and when you experience it, take it down and incorporate it. It will now be your truth."* Remember until you have experienced it for yourself, it will not be your truth nor will you be able to see as the truth. You use opinions to try to understand what your world is about until you have the experience that changes your view. It is only with experience that it will become a truth for you. So in essence it is fruitless to argue about what is not based on experience. You are arguing based on opinions or viewpoints. These are not truths. So it is pointless to argue. They are changeable.

Beliefs that limit us are those we take on that are based on what we were told is true, without any experience/s to back them up. We get these from our loved ones and from those we trust, through our religious beliefs systems, through society, how we were raised, and more. These beliefs are not based on any experience. They are based on the total reliance of someone you either loved or trusted. They told you it was true and you believed them. They didn't mean to mislead you. They were told the same thing as you. What they told you they really believed to be true themselves.

Maybe you thought at the time that they only wanted the best for you. They loved you so what they told you must be true. With that being said, you insert these beliefs into your belief system, remember they are not based on anything other than they love you or you trusted them and on the idea that they only want the best for you. You incorporated them. You need to question that and ask yourself, *"What if they are operating on a belief not based on experience too?"* These are the beliefs that limit you in some way. They are opinions only. Opinions are CHANGEABLE through your experiences.

Your opinion changes as you have the experience/s. This now become your truth but you must understand those who haven't had the experience yet, it *will not* be their truth. They have not reached that point in their perceptions.

Having opinions on anything creates closed mindedness, judgments, arguments, triggers, prejudices, and many more negative thoughts and actions. Truths on the other hand are those based solely on experience. They are UNCHANGEABLE.

Opinions are the weak joints in a foundational structure and will eventually crumble in time. Truths stand strong supported by your experiences. So if your beliefs, no matter what they are, are built on opinions and blind faith then your belief system will eventually crumble around you. Have you tried to convince someone who has this type of foundation to look at their limited beliefs? Don't try is all I can say. They are at such a low level of perception they won't see your point or perception anyway.

Base what you know on your experiences and you will find life becomes so much more positive. Once you start building a foundation on truths it cannot be shaken. All doubts and fears start to fade. We want only truths to build on. Clear all that you think you know except those acquired through your experiences. Build your foundation from here. On truths only.

This written information is based on my experiences with my own healing path. They are my truths and I want everyone to find their own truths through healing like I did. Don't take my word for it. For that matter don't take anyone's word. Find out for yourself. Experience the Divine on a personal level like I teach others. Proof will be your truth.

You will find that these concepts within this book will eventually be your truths too, some day. These types of truths will build a strong solid foundation. Remember nothing can shake this type of foundation apart. It will allow you to stand strong and weather anything life throws at you.

CHAPTER 18

ARGUING OR DISPUTES

When we argue we are generally arguing an opinion. Because if it were based on truth then there wouldn't be an argument. Each person is arguing a point that they *feel* is the truth. Maybe one knows the truth and the other one hasn't experienced it yet. But if one has the truth and they understand this concept they would *"turn the other cheek"* and walk away. I will tell you until they have the experience they will argue their point because they *FEEL* that it is the truth. Just remember it is the truth for them until they get the experience to make the change/s in their perception.

Let me put it this way to those of you who are arguing—you are technically right for where you are at in your perceptions. Whether it is based on opinions or truths. It doesn't matter. Everyone is technically right. No one really wins. So why are we arguing? We are arguing to be right. Therefore, arguing is pointless.

Truths do the opposite of what opinions do. They open your mind, stop the arguments, the disputes, there will be no triggers, no prejudices, and more. Plus, it will open your heart to what is real and genuine. They help you to create inner peace and expand your consciousness to higher levels of perception and much more.

We need to start with deprogramming ourselves. What do I mean by that? We are not taught how to think anymore we are told what to think. It is time to wake up. Start thinking for yourself. You just need to open the box up that we keep ourselves in and start thinking outside the box. You can't learn to think for yourself by following other people either. In essence it means getting rid of everything that is not yours and anything not based on *YOUR* experiences. It is starting all over again. Turn over every stone until you find what you need. Get rid of any beliefs that you have acquired and incorporated from others and anything else not based on an experience. Anything, that prevents you from manifesting what you want out of life. Only keep what you have experienced and build from there. Don't worry about being influenced. You already have been and just didn't know it. You just need to know the difference between what is right or wrong for you and go from there. Learn to think for yourself. Find your experiences and don't be afraid to seek them out.

When you get rid of your limited thoughts and beliefs you stop the arguing, the judgments and much more. You learn to accept people for who they are and not who you feel they should be based on your perceptions. You start freeing yourself from the chains that bind you to express yourself in a more enlightened manner.

CHAPTER 19

ALL TIME IS NOW

Linear time is time that flows in a straight or linear line. Linear time exist in our physical/conscious reality. It is created by man. Time is actually cyclical in nature which is a spiritual concept. A concept connected to our God/Unconscious mind. It is on the right side of our brain which is our spiritual side.

We also find that everything that is naturally created in nature has a circular shape to it. You will find this circular concept throughout Creation. With that being said all natural things in creation that are visible and touchable, like the trees etc. have this circular nature to them. The invisible and untouchable like the cycles of the day, seasons, the sun etc. All these have a circular spiritual time aspects connected to them.

Those things that are not seen like the movement of energy, our thoughts, karma, and much more travels in this circular manner. The old saying *"what goes around comes around,"* is in reference to this. That everything will make a full circle eventually. So keep this in mind. What you send out will come back around to you, the good as well as the bad. It will come back ten-fold.

Keeping with this thought that time is cyclical in nature simply means that the past and future is here right now in the present. It is constantly circling back around lifetime after lifetime. This is the concept that connects us to our karmic return and debt. This is what makes history repeat itself. This then makes us responsible for all our families' karma because we are energetically tied to them. We must deal with and heal our own past life karma and our ancestors karma. Wow! Now that is something to think about. We need to start healing ourselves as well as our ancestors to attain freedom from karmic debt. This being just one of the areas that needs clearing to help us achieve our goal of attaining enlightenment.

The following exercises I give to the students I teach to help them stay in the present, *'the Now'* which is a modern day concept. This includes a focusing and concentration exercise. One that requires monitoring your thoughts and where they are. Another one that uses all your senses. With practice you will become more and more aware and in the now plus it will increase your focus and concentration.

1. This exercise has been around forever. Don't know who started it but it works fantastic. Focusing and concentration requires picking something to focus on for ten minutes a day. I usually have the students use a white candle but you can use anything like a leaf, a dot on the wall, a spot on the floor, a plant, it can be anything. It is your choice. Have a pencil and paper with you and place tally marks on it without taking your eyes off the object of concentration. Place a mark on the paper when a thought comes in that isn't describing or pertaining to what you are focusing on. After a while you will begin to pick up some thoughts you never noticed before. For instance: You have the thought of what you choose to focus on. Then you have the tally mark thoughts (the ones that creep in out of nowhere). Then, what you really will begin to notice is the thoughts that creep in between the two thoughts after a while. These are the thoughts you really want to take notice of.

2. This one seems simple but requires constant awareness. It is watching what you are thinking constantly. This is difficult and I am not sure if anyone achieves too much success with this. But it puts you in the habit of monitoring your thoughts regularly. Where are your thoughts? What are you thinking of? Are you in the past? In the future? Or in the present? If you ask yourself these questions and keep yourself in the now or the present your

mind won't wander to the past and stay there nor will it stay in the future. You will eventually stay more and more in the now by bringing yourself to the present each time you catch yourself in the past or future. Exercise number three will also help you with this.

3. This is an old exercise too. Not sure of its origin either. This exercise starts incorporating your senses. In everyday chores or activities bring your senses into play and just begin noticing. For instance: if you are doing dishes really focus on the sense you chose to use first. Like touch. Actually put all your awareness in feeling whatever you are washing. Then move to the next sense. We will go to seeing. Really see yourself scrubbing, see the food being washed off, see the water, see the dish soap and the bubbles. What do they look like? I believe you have the idea of what I am after. So now do the other senses. If you do this regularly all your senses start to heighten. Make sure you go through all your senses. Do this regularly on a daily basis with all your activities.

CHAPTER 20

PAST, PRESENT AND FUTURE

So many people today live in the past. They do not know how to release the emotional scars or triggers that continually takes them back to the past. When this happens they keep triggering that emotional response over and over keeping them from living life in the present. They suffer with depression, deep sadness and many other mental issues. Eventually these will lead to physical illness. I will explain this from a healing place on how I came to understand this concept.

Hopefully the following example will put this in perspective. This is truly a hard concept to convey but I will do my best. Keep in mind that we are spirit/soul, mind and body. In order to manifest anything we need to be aware and that means body, mind and spirit must stay in the present.

Your energetic spirit is connected to all of you on all levels of your being including your mind. If your mind is in the past or the future then you are not in the present or what most call the now. You need to be in the present with all of your being. Meaning the spirit, mind and body must all be in the moment. It doesn't mean you can't go to the past or the future. You can visit them just don't live there. You can stop living there by finding an energetic healer that can override the imprint the emotion caused to begin with.

For your spiritual advancement, health, happiness, and all the other positive aspects in your life that you are wanting to manifest you will need to be able to stay in the now. One of the ways you can help yourself stay in the now is to become aware of your present environment. What is in your surroundings? Any activities going on around you at the time? Become *AWARE* of all things in your life. That way spirit/soul, mind, and body stay in the present.

This is an example of where most people are today. They are usually in the past and will dream a little bit in the future. Very seldom do they stay in the present or the Now.

Living in Past	Staying in the Present/Now	Visiting the Future
Spirit/Energy	Spirit/Energy	Spirit/Energy
Mind/thoughts	Mind/thoughts	Mind/thoughts
	Body	

This is where you need to be

Past	Present/Now	Future
	Spirit/Energy	
	Mind/thoughts	
	Body	

CHAPTER 21

OUR SCRIPTS OR STORIES

O ur stories are what we tell ourselves and others to describe to them who we are or who we want them to think we are. Just think about this. We live in the biggest theater ever built. We are all actors and actresses in this physical existence on the most beautiful stage ever created. We have chosen the roles that we play through our Divine contracts and through our free will choices. The problem is we want to cling to our stories from the past instead of releasing and healing them. The more we tell our stories. The more we act out our stories. The more we become our stories. Any repetitive story or thought will manifest when it is coupled with emotion, especially intense emotion. If you don't release these stories it will interfere with your Divine contract that you are here to fulfill in this lifetime.

Before I started teaching I did a healing on someone who later convinced me to teach class. The alternative healing method I used really woke him up. He called me after the healing and wanted to talk to me. He came to my house and told me stories about his bar days. How he drank and how didn't take any crap from anyone. Well if you could see this guy I wouldn't give him any crap to begin with. His stories focused on how big a bully he was and on how bad he could be. Well anyway that is how I saw him. So I stopped him after about a half-hour and said to him, *"Is this who you really are? A bully? I want to know who you really are. The one that is deep down inside. Who is he? This is the person I want to get to know not the one you want everyone to see or the one you think you are."* You see this is how he described who he was to me with his stories. This is how he saw himself. This is who he thought he was. This was what he was becoming. The more he told himself and others these stories the more he saw and became the person in those stories. He left after our talk and sometime later in the year he called me and asked me if I would teach classes. Eventually I did set up classes and I found the person I was looking for that night. The loving, kind, generous, big teddy bear person that I love dearly. This guy had the biggest epiphany of his life that day. With a few simple questions. It changed his whole life. Never doubt your part in this world to make a difference. Even if you feel it is minor it can make a huge impact on someone. Maybe it is just one kind simple word, or one kind simple sentence, or maybe an unconscious or conscious act of kindness that you gave to someone, that had a big life changing effect on them. If people would just do this, it would make a huge difference in our world today.

Just know the information contained inside this book is life changing if you are brave and courageous enough to look at yourself and be honest. This wasn't easy for this guy to do or anyone else who enters my class. This guy and my other students did this and it changed their lives.

My classes are difficult to take as well as difficult to teach. No one wants to be told how they are. I myself had a difficult time with healing because of this. I thought I couldn't be that way. That they must be wrong. Not true, I was in denial and they were right. All I know is, I wouldn't change my healing experiences for the world. No matter how difficult they were at the time. It has changed my life.

So what stories do you write or tell people, to try to express who you are to them? You need to ask yourself the following questions? Do you even know who you really are? What masks are you putting on and wearing? Find your stories and heal them. Find the message/s in them. Find the lesson/s in them. Then give thanks and gratitude for all that you have learned. Start being who you truly are and not what you think others want you to be.

Discard your old negative stories inside your book of life on how abused and mistreated you were. Of how you don't fit in. Throw away everything that you told yourself and what others THOUGHT you were to date, because these affect you too. Now is the time to start doing this. So you can be healthy, happy, and whole again. Rewrite your stories in a new book of life that has your name on it.

Once you start giving gratitude and finding the lessons you are here to learn you begin your healing journey. You can start a new chapter in your book. Write your stories through conscious participation and not the ones you unwittingly created or feel others have created for you. With this information you can do this. Write a story that is positive in nature and is based on who you really are deep down. Then you can begin manifesting what you really want in life. Start telling new more positive stories and manifest these instead.

CHAPTER 22

GIVING, RECEIVING, ENABLING AND OUTCOME

This is an area of misunderstanding too. There is more to generosity than the understanding we currently have. We are told to give to the poor. Help those who are in need. Whatever the case maybe. But most of us operate from a principle concerning this based on their understanding of karma, *"what goes around comes around"*. Hence, expecting a return or an outcome of some kind.

We really should give but give with a different definition than we currently have today of what giving is. We just need to do it without expecting anything in return. Give from your heart instead. We are constantly giving and giving to those who are around us, to various institutions, or organizations at our own detriment. We give even when we are not in a position to give. Where we actually suffer with the outcome of our giving in some way. Why? Because we lack the understanding of what true giving is.

It is one thing to give but it is another to expect some sort of outcome or return from your acts of giving. I am sure I am not telling you anything you *feel* you don't know here but I will give you a few examples toward the end of this section of what I really mean.

I want to touch lightly on what I hear from most people, when I asked them about giving. They used the following sayings, *"What goes around comes around, it is better to give than to receive and if you give you will receive it back tenfold."* These are all restrictive negative beliefs. They are preventing you from receiving Universally. Giving only works if you give without expecting a return of some kind. Be wary of those who promise you a return of some sort. This is where we have all misconceived the idea about the concept of giving. I am about to give you a different spin on things.

I have heard people say endlessly about how many times they have given and given to no avail. They are waiting for the Universe to respond tenfold. For example to be rich, to be healthy. They are expecting some sort of exchange. When they are asked to give a dollar to get ten dollars back most people will do this. When they do this however, and they get nothing in return, they don't understand why it didn't work.

Maybe you decided to give because you wanted to feel better. If you are expecting something in return this is not going to happen! That is not true giving. This is called bartering. True giving is the act of giving something from the heart without expectations of future benefits. Give because you want to give and not because someone asked you to. Maybe they told you to give to reserve a place in the afterlife. This is still bartering. This is not how true giving works!

I know people who give others their last dollar when they need it for themselves. Don't give if you don't have it to give. You need to ask yourself why you are doing this because it certainly isn't helping your cause any. Maybe you thought it was the right thing to do. Or maybe you didn't want them to go without something. What's up with this concept? If you did this you need to ask yourself what role you are playing. You could also search within yourself to find out what benefits you are receiving from it. Maybe you are trying to be a martyr, a hero, or want some sort of praise to make yourself feel better about something. The point is, if this is the reason for giving then again you have given for the wrong reasons. You are expecting a return of some sort. This type of giving increases your stress and makes you miserable. So you give to make someone else happy and you do without. You take on their suffering. You are now unhappy because now you need someone to give to you. For some reason I have trouble with this type of reasoning. How about you?

This type of giving is not solving any of your problems or theirs for that matter. It is only making things worse for everyone involved. It puts you in an imbalanced state and exposes you to dis-ease within your energetic field. There is a definite imbalance today concerning this issue. The bottom line is if you *have it* and *want to give* then please do. Just remember to give from your heart only and don't expect anything in return and you will be much happier. You will find the Universe will start responding to you. Through the true definition of giving. Which must contain the word *SELFLESS* in it.

If this is not practiced then the positive act of giving is met with a negative act of resentment, for example, because you are not getting the return for your kindness from the Universe you feel you deserve. Remember this is not true giving and this cancels the good will of the act. So you haven't gained or accomplished anything. It was a waste of your time and energy and created stress for you.

Receiving is also in a state of imbalance today with people. We have those who take and take and take and never give anything in return. They feel it is owed to them. They will do anything to get you to give to them. They take advantage of you through your interpretation of helping by using deception.

Then we have those who give and give but have trouble receiving. Then we have those who don't give or receive at all. All of these are imbalances that need to be brought to awareness and healed. This not only applies to individuals but it also applies to organizations and institutions. Greed has consumed the world. Where does it end? It will end when we decide to start waking up by being more aware of what is really going on around us and by balancing and healing these issues within us first. Remember we cannot get rid of our negative aspects but we do need to balance them within us. We do this by being aware of them as we go through life.

In order to balance these we must learn the true act of giving as well as receiving *without* any *conflicting emotions and without a benefit of some sort that we feel we deserve in return*. When you can do this you are well on your way to truly understanding giving and receiving. Being able to do this will enable you to heal deeply at a spiritual/energetic level. I will give to you the few examples I have encountered within my life to possibly give you a better explanation. To be honest I can only touch on a few points concerning this. Just like everything else there is always more to see if you decide to look deeper.

1. I hear so many people say, *"I constantly help them out and this is how I get treated"*! Or *"this is what I get in return"*! Here are a few statements that definitely shows that they gave free willingly but they expected future returns of some sort. Maybe it was to get some respect, or did they give to get loyalty, or maybe a bit of recognition. It states they expected some sort of future benefits from their act of giving. Just remember this is a one-sided agreement that you made without the other person's knowledge. So when the other person doesn't give them what they feel they deserved for giving or helping it creates a negative situation. The giver became indignant toward the other person. You are to blame for this, not them. Just keep this in mind. If you wanted something in return you should have stated what you wanted up front so they can agree to the exchange. But, if you do this then it is not true giving. Remember, this is called bartering.

2. Then there are institutions and organizations who make you feel guilty if you don't give. Or they promised you a return of some kind on your act of giving. Like redemption or a reserved spot after your death. You can't buy yourself a place in the afterlife. Sorry it just doesn't happen. No one can promise that. Nor can they promise you atonement of any kind *"only if you would just give to the cause"*. Start taking responsibility for your own soul cleansing. We need to stop waiting for the answers that will not come by relying on others to give them to you. Start searching yourself! This book will help you with this because I do understand the answers you are seeking are not being given or taught in the places you are frequenting. That is why I am writing this to give you a direction. Just know beyond a shadow of a doubt that no one can save your soul but you. That my friend is your job only! No priest or preacher can do that for you. Think about that. How can they?

3. Giving makes you feel better not them. But what about those you give to, who you *enable* with your giving. You are actually doing more harm than good and you are not helping them at all.

This is such a touchy situation. But hopefully, I will put this into perspective too. It doesn't matter if it is a relative of yours and you feel you need to help them because they are down on their luck, *"because that is what friends and families do."* This is a restrictive belief. Maybe you feel all they need is that extra boost to get them going in the right direction. You may even just feel sorry for them. What if it is just you that feels this way and not them? What if they are not ready to change their life because they like themselves and their life just as it is? You are the one who thinks they are not happy, or they need more in their life just to name a few for instances. So hence, they are not going to change or do better. We need to stop thinking this will make them feel better. They are actually taking advantage of your good will and you are enabling them to continue their behavior. This is where they deceived you or you deceived yourself into thinking they need help. Here again we are expecting a return from those we give to. Just remember this holds true and it is not limited to people only. Included in here is any charitable agencies, organizations, and institutions. Beware of the return in all giving.

Stop with the expectations of a return or an outcome of some sort when you do any positive act. Expecting something in return cancels out any positive you have done. Look at the situation to see if you are enabling the person/s you think you are helping. Release the expectations you place upon yourself and others. Give from your heart without any expectations of any kind and the Universe will start responding to you with true giving.

CHAPTER 23

LABELS

I sn't it funny how we label things? I understand we need to do this to keep organized in our physical environment but I am not talking about this type of labeling. I am referring to how we label people for one. Our stories also create labels. We label ourselves as well as others who label us. Why? Do you want to be labeled? Of course not. When we label we are judging. We are making ourselves more superior than that person. For instance that person is untrustworthy. Maybe that person is evil. We are all untrustworthy and evil to a certain degree. Well let me tell you we are all equal in this area. No one is above and no one is below anyone else. We need to start accepting others for who they are and not for who we think they should be. They were created the same as you were. We all possess the same attributes. We need to stop this insanity. This is affecting people emotionally, mentally, and physically. Not only that, but it contributes to the anger and violence we see today.

The roles and labels we give ourselves come from our little theater of life. They come from the stories we tell ourselves and from others who label us. For instance: I am a mother. A label. I am a healer. A label. A label can be positive or negative. What labels do you give yourself to describe you? What labels do others place on you? What labels do you place on other people? Why do we even need labels? Think about these questions. Labels keep us restricted and prevent us from expanding our consciousness. From being happy, healthy, whole and much more. Let's stop the labeling.

One of my students asked me one day what I called myself. I laughed because she was finally seeing the picture. Then she asked if I could describe what I did. My answer to this was, *"I don't know how to explain it. It just is"*. I have never figured out how to describe what I do. This book can't even explain it. I'm trying but I think I am failing. The problem I have is I don't see labels anymore I see everyone on their own Divine journey whether it is a 'positive or negative' journey which I don't see as negative or positive anymore. Either way it is a journey they choose with the Divine before they were born and then given free will to fulfill it.

There are several reasons we are here. One of the reasons we are here is to learn lessons and to experience. Another reason we are here is to clear karma. Our own and our ancestors. Keep in mind these are not the only reasons.

Chapter 24

ENERGY

When I took biology in college I learned the three characteristics of energy, which are:

1. It is already here.
2. It CANNOT be destroyed.
3. It CAN be transformed.

There is One Energy that permeates and forms everything in Creation and it is called Divine/Creator Energy. This energy is found in every aspect of our energetic/spiritual makeup and physical reality. This includes the unseen that is around us or in other words what we call space which science considered at one time to be void of any matter. Just because we can't see it doesn't mean the space around us is empty. It is filled with Divine Energy. It is from this One Source of energy that another energy is found that makes up our physical existence and it is found in the space around us as well. If there is only One Source of energy that created everything where did the second one come from? It is the transformed energy of the Creator. Still comes from this One Source we call Creator it is just transformed. Thus creating another type of energy. A heavier denser type of energy.

1. The first Energy is Creator/Divine energy it contains the first and second characteristics of energy, it already exist and cannot be

destroyed. From an energetic or spiritual perspective we have Light Divine Energy which is positive energy. This energy is composed of both male and female energetic vibrations. We too are made of and possess both male and female energetic aspects. Everything in creation has male and female energies in its make-up. It is the unconditional loving energy of the Creator that is referred to as God, Goddess, Lord, Lady, Universe, Source, Great Spirit, Holy Ghost, and more.

There are seventy-two different names to identify this energy such as Buddha, Christ, Muhammad and more. There are over ten thousand different names to describe the feminine energies of the Creator such as the Virgin Mary, Isis, Dianas, and Mother Earth just to name a few. To achieve this connection to the Divine source of energy is the goal we are all striving for and is referred to by many as achieving Bliss, Grace, Nirvana, Heaven and more.

From a physical perspective this energy creates everything that is natural in Creation. Like the trees, animals, grass, all things we see that is untouched by humans. Everything that is naturally here including humans. These are Divine creations. Created from the refined energy of Divine thoughts.

2. It cannot be destroyed. It is here and will always be here. This is self-explanatory.
3. This is where the third characteristic of energy falls, it can be transformed. Remember it can't be destroyed. From a spiritual/ energetic perspective this is the heavier or gray, dark energy which is *negative* or what is considered bad energy. *This is also the energy of the Creator that has been transformed.* This is what we humans use to create what some traditions refer to as *evil* energy. Some call it Hell or something similar in other traditions. To me this is a catch all word for what is not good. We take the One Source of energy that is in existence and transform this Divine energy with our negative actions, thoughts, and behaviors through our chakras, our emotions and nervous system. ***This type of energy is ONLY created by humans. This is important to remember.*** We

take the Light of the Creator and transform it into what we term as *evil*. This is the original *SIN* we have committed and continue to commit because we lack the understanding of how we have *sinned* to begin with. So I am giving it to you. Stop using Divine Energy and transforming it by doing *bad* things. If we do this we could stop all the wrong that we see in the world. We can live in peace, balance, and harmony.

Remember there is only One Source of energy that creates everything, even the negative energy. We take the Light Divine Loving Creator Energy, and transform it into something that is bad or negative spiritually/energetically. This is the *sin* they say we have done. We are able to do this because of our Divine Essence or Spark of Divine Light that makes us all children of the Creator. We all possess a Divine spark or Light of the Creator that gives us the ability to create also. Maybe in a less powerful way of what the Creator can do but we can create none-the-less. This energy is referred to by some as evil, negative, bad and more. The old saying that states there is always a spark of light even in darkness holds true because of this concept.

We go to our spiritual leaders to be cleansed (absolved) of our *sins* and most of us don't even know what they mean by that. It is something we are supposed to do and told to do. So we do it. Hence, control. I don't think they even know what they mean by that. We just accept it because they know more than we do! Remember? So we go and we ask for forgiveness over and over again for the same *sins* because we aren't sure what *sins* are. We just think it is doing bad things. That is not all it is. Learn from your mistakes if you don't then you are *sinning* and you will need absolution because you haven't learned yet how not to *sin*. It is a vicious cycle that we need to stop. So learn from your mistakes. Stop doing negative things.

Start forgiving yourself or others for their mistakes. Once you learn from your mistakes and you don't repeat the *sin* you will then be able to move closer to enlightenment. All you need is your own forgiveness and the understanding of what your *sins* are. When you understand this you are well on your way to clearing your path to the Divine. Total enlightenment like the Masters of the past.

Sins in an energetic/spiritual sense is all the things we may call bad or negative that we feel or sense, maybe even see around us. This can and does include dis-eases that manifest in our energetic fields as vibrational imprints. These vibrational imprints affect our spiritual, physical, mental, and emotional levels. These energies are created by our emotional responses and made manifest through our nervous system. I will explain more on this this later.

You must understand that the degree of what is referred to as negative or bad depends on the person, their experiences, their perspective, their emotional state, and many other factors which are individually based. In other words what some may consider as devastating or bad for them may not be considered as devastating or bad to someone else.

These two types of energy (Divine and Transformed by humans) which can also be seen as two different conditions of consciousness.

1. Divine energy—this level consist of the Energy we call Creator. It is Light energy of the Creator which is a very refined energy. It has the highest of vibrations and the lightest of densities. It is a very ordered energy. Located on the right side of the brain. It is our unconscious or spiritual existence.

Higher Level: this consist of Divine Spiritual energy also known as Higher Astral, Higher Mental, Higher Self, Higher Level, Celestial Dragon, Heaven, Upper World, subconscious, unconscious, and is connected to our energetic or spiritual self.

2. Transformed by humans—this level consist of the energy created by humans. It is heavy sometimes called "dark" energy with low vibrations and densities. Very chaotic disordered energy. Located on left side of brain. Our conscious physical existence.

Other names for this type are Lower Mental, Lower Astral, Lower Self, Lower Level, Terrestrial Dragon, Hell, Underworld, our consciousness, and is connected to our physical reality. The name used depends on your belief system or school of thought.

The astral is actually the realm of the mental mind. So to simplify things I will use the mental mind in this book (sometimes referred to as the mental/emotional mind) because this is what you are familiar with just understand there are many levels within levels.

As you have seen the two conditions of our consciousness is divided today into what we call the conscious and un/subconscious minds. These are the terms we are most familiar with when we connect the spiritual/ energy part of ourselves to our physical part. I believe that we have one consciousness. We divided this consciousness when we started using and transforming Divine energy. This is what made our consciousness split. Creating what we call the Ego. When we did this we created our separation from the Creator. The conscious and the subconscious minds need to work together to inform each other so we can receive our spiritual or energetic messages. We need to be able to receive these messages in our physical or conscious existence. Whether we hear or receive these or not depends on how spiritual you are.

How big a separation you have created is based on how negative or positive you are. How big your Ego is. How much into self you are. This determines our Creator access. When we divided our consciousness (which is our physical reality) by choosing to be more negative than positive. We created a separation within us from our Creator (our spiritual/energy part) which is known as the unconscious or subconscious part of ourselves every time we choose the negative.

We created a division with the creation of our lower level consciousness. Remember our lower level conscious realm is created by taking the energy of the Creator and transforming it with our negative thoughts, actions, behaviors, etc. Hence, we *left* the proverbial Garden through our free will when we did this. This is when we stopped listening and hearing the messages from the Higher Vibrational Realms, from our Creator. We lowered our vibrations by doing and practicing the negative. We became 'lost' so to speak. To get back to the Garden we have to reverse what we have done by transforming the negative. Practicing Divine spiritual practices regularly will lead us Home again to the Garden.

In esoteric belief systems the physical body is seen as an upside down tree with the roots on top. It is also symbolic of the reflections of the world's. We see this in the Lord's Prayer, *"let it be done on Earth as it is in*

Heaven", also in the phrase, *"As above, so Below"*. Here again we see the two modes of consciousness and types of energies connected to them. Earth, the human physical element. Heaven, the spiritual energetic aspect of ourselves. Hopefully you are getting the picture of how we are spiritual and physical. We are the embodiment of both modes. We are spiritual first and foremost because of our Divine essence and we must start being more spiritual by putting this level first in all that we do. When you are negative in what you do you are practicing the lower level mode of consciousness not the higher level perceptions of the Creator so keep this in mind.

Thoughts:

You have heard the phrase "thoughts are things". This means that whatever you think will manifest in your life. This happens because of your Divine essence especially if you couple it with intense emotion. Just know you are the creator of everything that is good or bad in your life. Through your free will choices. You manifest what you think including the emotions attached to what you want. Try to make good choices and watch your negative thoughts. Clear up your energy field. Remember you become what you think. If you feel your life is bad then it will be bad or vice-verse. Remember your stories? They are energy too. Just like your thoughts. They will manifest.

Today in most of our lives we have a lot of anxieties and stress. We are constantly in a state of worry where we think about money, health, jobs, children, relationships and more. You need to consider the fact that the anxieties and stress you have will manifest too. The Law of Attraction also works in manifesting the negative as I have described. Think about where your thoughts are. I am sure this information will help you cope better with everyday living decreasing your stresses and worries plus get you more Divinely Connected. Truthfully, I want this information to help you manifest the life you want which is free of anxieties and stress.

CHAPTER 25

OUR ENERGETIC FIELD, OUR AURA AND SPIRIT BODY

Everyone has an energy field that surrounds them that is electromagnetic in nature. It has many colors within it that are always changing. The colors within this field change according to your mood, stress levels, your emotional states, physical health, just to name a few. It connects and extends from your body to about the distance of your outstretched arms. There are filaments of light that extend and connect to everything in creation. We are constantly exchanging energy with everything and everyone in our environment and with all of creation through our energetic field. It is an act of exchange, of giving and receiving, of reciprocity with all of Creation.

Our electromagnetic nature is created from the Earth's North and South Poles and our connection to them. This is our magnetic nature and is connected to the water in our bodies. The electrical part of field is connected to the Earth and to the East and West Cardinal Points. This is connected to our nervous system which is the element of fire in our body. There is more to this but I want to diagram the rest under the Caduceus section and show you how the spiritual/energetic part of us works within our body and energetic layers.

The way the energy flows in and out of the body is similar to the flow of energy between two magnets. It is also the same flow of energy that the

Earth has as it flows through the poles. It flows up from the bottom of your feet through the spinal column and out through the top of the head through the crown. Then it flows back down to the Earth to start the same process all over again. This creates our energy field around our body. Our electromagnetic field. This is the same flow the Earth has around her. Earth also has an electromagnetic field around it. We are a reflection of the Earth in every part of our makeup.

Your spiritual energetic field around you is connected to and held to your body via the chakras. Upon death the chakras release your energy field and the energy in the body so you can cross over to the other side. The chakras run the length of your spine with the upper two chakras located in the head area. There are many excellent books on the market that are written on the chakras. I will touch lightly on these but I would suggest you find a book that you like, to get more information describing the function of each one if you want. It's always a good idea to get knowledge to add to any information you may have on these.

Chakra is a Sanskrit word that means wheel of light. Spinning vortexes of Light that are cone shaped. We have seven major chakras that brings good energy into the body. They help to discharge negative energy from the body. Our body acts as a capacitor and a transformer of energy. We are able to regulate the energy being brought in or released out of the body through the chakras. Chakras can be viewed as large bolts that holds the energy field to our body. They bring in or release energy in our bodies by the clockwise spin or counterclockwise spin.

There are so many sites out there describing the chakras that I will not add any more information about them. Just put chakras in your search bar and all sorts of information will appear.

We also have streams or rivers of light as I have heard them called that run along the surface of our skin that help bring and feed energy into the body. These streams are connected to each other with junctions called meridians. You can view these as smaller minor chakras. These minor chakras are the junctions for these streams of light to connect to each other. Some traditions have charted these and have found over eighty-eight thousand of them. These junctions are what acupuncturist use to clear out blocks within our energetic/spiritual field that create blockages or problems within our bodies.

When we place our hands together in prayer we are actually opening the ten acupuncture meridians that run the length of our body from toe to head. Prayer position provides the access to the opening of these ten spiritual/energy lines or channels to provide that direct connection to Creator.

There are many ways to remove blockages other than acupuncture if you have an issue with this method. All you have to do is research and you will find a lot of alternative healers that can do this. Spiritual/Energy healers. They can remove the energy for you. Once removed you still must keep it from returning. You can call it back to you. Because you have an affinity to that energy or you wouldn't have had it in your energy field to begin with. You do this by changing or healing the problem or emotion that brought it in to begin with.

CHAPTER 26

THE STAFF OF LIFE

The Staff of Life is a very ancient symbol which is known as: The Caduceus, the Staff of Moses, the Staff of Hermes, Hermes Magic Wand, the Staff of Asclepius, Asclepius is Apollo's son. Just to name a few.

The Staff of Life is seen on ambulances, Doctor's attire, anywhere that represents health and in the medical field, medicine. There are tons of variations to depict this ancient symbol. I have drawn a few—(*See figures 1 and 2 at the back of book*) at the end of the book. The Caduceus describes the interaction between the physical body and its health with its energetic/spiritual counterparts. It shows our connection between our conscious and unconscious minds. The interaction of all these determines our overall state of well-being. The terminology may be different or the depiction of the symbol just keep in mind the information never changes.

The Caduceus is much more then I may even be aware of. But I figured out a lot of its meaning and function. For the health care professionals it is the healing that occurs with someone who is ill on the physical level. For me it represents the spiritual/energetic nature of all illnesses or disease on all levels—the physical, spiritual, emotional, and mental levels. All these levels must work together to achieve optimal health, happiness, wholeness, etc. They must be kept in equilibrium to keep healthy. Today these areas have been separated into sections. Like the medical, psychiatric, spiritual or energetic end. The problem is we can't separate these. If we want optimal health on all levels.

I have laid some groundwork on energy earlier in this book hopefully it is enough and done in enough layman terms to give you an understanding of how important the energetic side is to all illnesses. I am hoping you will see what I am trying to describe concerning disease and illness and how it relates to the body. I want to show how our emotions are connected to all our physical, mental, emotional, and spiritual issues. Thus blocking what you may want to manifest in your life when you have negative emotions.

As I said earlier every area of health and healing is separated. In reality there is no separation. The Staff of Life will show this. One area always affects the other. So why separate? Money? I don't know. It is my opinion there shouldn't be any separation of these. They go hand in hand. So how can they be separated? Hopefully I can convey this in this article. If not, all I can say is I tried. I believe this is where modern medicine has dropped the ball. Hopefully I can covey this in the next several drawings and pages of text.

Remember I acquired this information from my personal experiences and this is how I put it together. I am not a psychologist, doctor, a counselor of any kind. I am an ordinary person on a spiritual journey that wants to help others gain health, happiness, enlightenment and so much more. I am advanced spiritually. To what degree I don't know, it really doesn't matter. I haven't reached the point of total enlightenment yet. I want to. I just haven't achieved it. I just wanted some sort of reason as to why I was dying and no one seemed to have the answers that I needed. I did my own research and developed a theory founded from my own personal knowledge and experiences. I placed the knowledge I gained from it on the Caduceus and found the missing keys I needed for my health. It did what I needed it to do. I am healthy. These keys will also help you.

I know that if you are reading this without judgment with an open heart you can see the benefit of this information. This will change how modern medicine, psychology, science, religion, and any other areas of interest view illness and disease today. By using knowledge that the Ancients knew about. Information that we have long forgotten. I am hoping this will revive interest and studies from the different fields interested in this subject. Hopefully someone will build upon this information and create a health and wellness system that incorporates all these areas of health as a plan for healing. A complete plan for healing without separating these fields. To truly study the effects coming from all levels of being and making it a cohesive *integrated system of wholeness* for complete health.

CHAPTER 27

THE ANCIENT SYMBOL
CALLED THE CADUCEUS

The Caduceus is everything. It is connected to everything. It is our key to health and happiness as well as our illnesses and sadness. It is what creates our life through our thoughts, emotions, actions, behaviors, etc...

It is the elements. It represents Earth, Air, Fire, Water and Spirit. The Wings are Air and connected to our Higher Self. The central shaft is Earth which symbolizes our spinal column and our physical manifestation. The two serpents are Fire and Water. This means it is also connected to the Medicine Wheel/Sacred Circle in Native American Spiritually and found in other spiritual beliefs. The ball at the top is our connection to our spiritual side and our Moon-eye. Spirit connects them to All of Creation through our energy fields. *(See figure 4 at the back of book).*

It is our connection/s to what we call the other worlds. Upper, Lower, and Middle Worlds. The Lower or Underworld is located on the right side of the brain. It is our consciousness. It is our conscious connection to our visible world or seen world and the energy connected here. The left side of our brain represents the Upper or Higher World. This is the location of our unconscious. It is our invisible world or unseen world of energy. Some call it our spirit world. This is our God connection. Our Middle World is our physical world. It represents both the seen and unseen worlds through our conscious and unconscious minds. This connection to both the visible and invisible worlds is our physical body. *(See figure 3 at the back of book)*.

The serpent energy is located at the tailbone. It is called serpent energy because it is coiled and resting there. The Caduceus shows us what our physical reality seeped in duality means. *(See figures 5 and 6 at the end of the chapter)*. So when out of balance *(as I will show later)* this can create mental/emotional and physical problems for us.

Keep in mind it doesn't matter what term/s you use just know it is all connected culturally, spiritually, philosophically, etc. to all information concerning health, spiritual enlightenment, mental/emotional issues and much more. It all has the same meaning and function regardless of the word/s used.

As you go I will describe and display the attributes that are both electrical and magnetic in nature. Also, male and female should not be viewed as genders. But seen as more descriptive in terms of male and female qualities. For example, female energies are considered any force that is receptive and male energies/forces are seen as active. Light and dark are not to be viewed as good or evil. Just light and heavy energies or positive and negative energies. I also have to separate the energies but keep in mind each possess positive and negative energies, electromagnetic energies, and male and female energies. There is no separation. I did this to simplify things.

The Shaft of the Caduceus is your spinal column and the circle at the top is your brain. Keep in mind the right side of your brain controls the left side of your body and the left side of your brain controls the right side of your body. The serpent energy crosses at your chakras as it moves up your spinal column which is represented by the shaft of the Caduceus. *(See figures 7 and 8 at the back of book)*. One serpent is black which depicts the negative. The other serpent is white which depicts positive. Both of these are known as our polarity. What we have on our right side of the body switches to the left side of the brain. The left side of our body and its attributes will switch and connect to the right side of our brain.

Remember we get our magnetism from our energetic connections to the North and South Poles. Our electrical aspect comes from our connections to the energies found in the East and West directions.

As I explain remember there is only ONE ENERGY that comprises everything. Science calls it energy. Spiritual beliefs call it Creator. It is made up of both male and female energies just like you possess both male and female energies. All I have done is separate that energy to show you how it works within our body, mind and spiritual aspects. To show how one affects the other. But it is one energy operating on different vibrations and having different densities. I separated the densities as heavy/negative—energy with weight. As light/positive—energy without any weight. Remember we create the heavy/negative energy. We maintain or increase our light/positive energies that are in our body, mind, and soul by controlling the negative.

The Twin Serpents/Dragons are also known as Kundalini Serpent Energy or Dragon Energy. The Yin and Yang. It represents the duality in our 3D world, our physical reality.

We each have two currents of energy that rest on either side of the central channel in the spinal column that houses our nervous system. They are seen as coiled and dormant until they are awakened and they start an energetic (electrical) flow of energy up the spine. This can be dangerous because if released too quickly without proper energetic clearing it can create a lot of unpleasant physical, mental, emotional issues, and possibly even death. Do not do any activation of any kind without the proper instructor and instructions.

These energies dwell in the 3rd eye area of the head. They are said they will grant great spiritual powers, (psychic abilities) health, and more. But they can also grant negative experiences, health issues, and more too. So before working with this energy do your RESEARCH! It is beneficial to you, to do so. A paper or a book cannot cover all the pitfalls, dangers, etc. connected to this energy if activated prematurely.

It doesn't matter what term/s you use just know it is all connected culturally, spiritually, philosophically, etc. to all information concerning health, spiritual enlightenment, mental/emotional issues and much more. It all has the same meaning and function regardless of the terms used.

THE FOLLOWING CHARTS LABELED *FIGURES 5 AND 6* SHOWS OUR WORLD OF DUALITY AND OPPOSITES IN OUR PHYSICAL AND SPIRITUAL REALMS—OUR VISIBLE WORLD- OUR PHYSICAL REALITY-AND OUR INVISIBLE WORLD OF SPIRIT AND ENERGY

BRAIN AND BODY
(Figure 5)

Energies connected to: Spiritual Self **RIGHT SIDE** OF **BRAIN—** **GOD-MADE**	Energies connected to: Physical **LEFT SIDE** OF **BRAIN—** **MAN-MADE**
Spirituality (Nature)	Religion (Organized Belief Systems)
Soul	Ego
Female/Yin	Male/Yang
CREATOR/GOD MIND— "I AM" CENTERED MIND — "For the benefit of All!" Mind	"ME" centered— "IT'S ALL ABOUT ME" — "For the benefit of Self mind"
Invisible World of Energy/Spirit	The Visible World of our Physical Reality
The *Unconscious Mind* our Spiritual/Energetic Aspects	The *Conscious Mind* our physical reality
Moon/Lunar (Lunar Consciousness)	Sun/Solar (Solar Consciousness)
Future	Past
The element Water	The element Fire
Magnetic—water is magnetic. so therefore will manifest our desires by using our emotions to magnetize the water in our body— with either good/positive or bad/negative emotions to create everything involved in our lives.	Electrical—is connected to our nervous system/s once the emotions magnetizes the water in our body— our nervous system kicks in to manifest what you want or desire through our emotions.
Darkness (hence Moon connection)	Light (hence Sun Connection)
Houses our intuitive Spiritual "Creator" side/connection	Our logical, rational aspects of of ourselves
To Be (Passive)	To Do (Action)
Passive	Active

CONTINUED BRAIN AND BODY
(Figure 6 continuation of figure 5)

- Emotion=Magnetism=Water .... Fire=Electrical=Nervous System
- Giving.. Receiving
- Stress=Emotion .... Flow=Nervous System
- Exhalation .... Inhalation
- Time.. Space
- Death Giving.............................. Life Giving
- Negative polarity......................... Positive polarity
- Fate/Destiny connected to .... Free Will (the ability to make patterns imprinted with your own choices) emotions already in the Mental/Emotional Mind

EGO—
ego rest in the center and flows back and forth
between the two sides of the brain.
Acting as an electromagnetic circuit/bridge to
connect the two consciousness's (between
your consciousness or physical self and your God Mind or Unconscious).
You can't receive any Divine messages however if you are stuck
in the "ME" centered side of your consciousness. The Ego quits
accessing the God side of your brain/mind when you have a "ME"
centered sense of self which exist mostly in the physical realm.

CHAPTER **28**

LANGUAGE AND BEING POSITIVE

O nce you have read the information you can start to divide the positive and negative in everything that you do. Like your actions, speech, behaviors, etc. to really open your eyes to see who and what you are saying. First step though is you must truly want to change, heal and to OWN your own stuff. *AWARENESS, HONESTY, and COURAGE* on your part is how you do this. Knowing when you are doing it. Catching yourself and changing it. Start being responsible for your actions, words, behaviors, etc. In order to start accessing the God Side of the brain. You must know what you are doing. I have already described several things that you could to do earlier in the book...like stop lying, learn the art of true giving, and practice staying in the Now. You should implement the practices I have mentioned earlier in almost every section of this book.

Language is another area where we falter. So let's take a look at this area.

If you want to know if you are being positive you can break your words down into your positive and negative aspects in your sentences. Divide a piece of paper in half. One side for positive/right brain/subconscious the other for the negative/left brain/conscious. Remember we live in a world of duality. Everything has an opposite. Set your example up with words that you want to use and their duality.

See example below to get an idea of what I am saying:

OPPOSITES/DUALITY
(WHERE DO YOU LIVING OR EXISTING?)

NEGATIVE-CONSCIOUS-YOUR PHYSICAL WORLD	POSITIVE-UNCONSCIOUS SIDE-GOD MIND
Physical body._____	Spirit or Energy Body.
Evil-bad-sinful. Ungodly Side._____	God Side-good-Divine acts.
Hate_____	Love
Never_____	Always
Connected to physical reality mind._____	Connected to God Mind.
Connected to "self"._____	Connected to Universal Mind.
Wish._____	Have.
Judgments_____	Acceptance
Punishment-Grudge_____	Forgiveness
Meanness-Indifference_____	Compassion
Rumors and Gossiping_____	Minding your own business.

Any words that are contractions:

Can't_____	Can
Don't_____	Do

Example: "*I wish I had a car*". Find the negative word or words. In this case it is wish and had. If you can put your words into past and future categories. Keep in mind, your conscious mind is connected to your past and your unconscious mind is connected to your future. See *(figures 5 and 6)* at the back of the book to help you understand.

Once you categorize your words then restate your sentence to make a more positive statement. Here is what you should have said, "*I have a car*". This statement takes it to the future that is connected to your God Mind. Put feeling to it and let the Universe know to manifest it for you. Simple? No. It takes practice and patience. You need to try and do this on a regular basis. Using words connected to the past from your conscious mind in a sentence, for the Creator to hear, will not be heard. The God

Mind, is connected to the future and will not recognize past tense words from your conscious mind self. These are considered negative words. Your God Mind only recognizes positive words. Words made of Light energy. If you say *"I will never do that again,"* then you are telling your God Mind... *"I will do that again".* If most of you have paid attention I would bet you have already experienced this. The old saying, *"Never say never",* as Charles Dickens said, fits nicely here.

Start staying in the Now and becoming AWARE of what you are thinking, saying, doing, etc. at all times. Begin saying sentences that are positive leaving out negative words. Remember the negative words are not recognized by the God Mind/Unconscious.

If you are living most of the time only in your conscious physical reality then you will be "ME" centered. Meaning *"it's all about me."* How many of you know people like this? Most of the world is already at this point today. The world revolves only around them. They are stuck in their consciousness, their physical life. They use very little of their God Mind. They can't really because they speak in negatives. I am sure you know people like this.

However, if we practice non-attachment and work on being humble *(this controls the ego)* we could eventually get rid of the ego. You can begin bridging the left side of your brain, your physical reality with the right side of your brain, your "God" part of Self to each other so you can receive the messages intended for you from the Creator. When we are "Me" centered then we have separated ourselves from our true connection to our Creator, which is our Universal Mind/God/Mind connection.

When you're angry, you're hurt, sad, when you treat others badly, get sucked up in dramas, use people etc. you are bringing in heavy negative/evil/bad energy. We can only heal if we are positive because this is what brings in the Light Divine Energy needed to raise our vibrations. Remember there are only two types of energy and we create the negative heavy energy by transforming Light/Divine energy into heavy energy with our anger, sadness, with all things negative. When you create heavy negative energy you are creating in your life the following—unhappiness, bad luck, illnesses, disease on the physical, mental, emotional, spiritual/ soul levels, lack of abundance, you seem stuck and much more. If you are experiencing any of these and life seems to suck then you are manifesting your negative. It also means you are carrying around a lot of heavy negative energy. The only way to reverse this is to transform the negative by being positive in all areas of your life. It is not easy, but ask yourself this, how long did it take you to get where you are today?

You could find someone who can remove it out of your energy field to transform it for you. You must be diligent in finding and changing what is negative about you so you can walk in Grace. So the Universe will Bless you again. When this is achieved then you will be able to walk in this life happy, healthy, with gratitude, abundance and much much more.

Just remember that as you study the following drawings try to make as many connections as you can. I had to separate the duality/opposites of the energies we hold within ourselves in order to explain them. Each negative has a little positive in it. Each positive has a little negative in it. This is the Yin and Yang. The Yin and Yang represents male and female energies and this is found in all energies. Again, just know there is no separation. Both sides are electromagnetic, both are male and female like the Yin and Yang means. There is a little of both energies *(the male and female, the electromagnetic components, etc.)* in each and all energies.

CHAPTER 29

EGO

Interaction and integration between the two sides or hemispheres of the brain can only be achieved by getting rid of Ego or 'ME' and developing a Universal Mind 'GOD Mind'. The *"for the benefit of all"* mind. This is where the saying comes in *"be humble"*. Being humble allows you to access your Creator Mind.

Place the Staff of Life between these two charts so you can see where and how these energies are represented. These charts show the left and right sides or hemispheres of your brain and what energies are located there. The circle at the top of Staff of Life is where the brain is shown. This also represents the Moon-Eye (*our spiritual connection to the physical world)* or 3rd Eye Chakra area. The Column on the Staff of Life represents your spinal column.

Now keep in mind the right side of your brain controls the left side of your body and the left side of your brain controls the right side of your body. This means everything that I have listed that are on the left side of your brain are now switched and are place in the lower half of your body on the right side of your body. Same goes for the right side of your brain. Everything listed here on the right side of your brain is now located on the left side of your body.

How this works is very difficult to explain but I will give it a try. This is why I keep repeating information for you to keep in mind. I feel as though I have given you enough information to understand a lot of what

I am about to write. Now, a few reminders. Do not see negative, dark, etc. as evil. See it as heavy dense energy that creates sickness, dis-ease, anything we consider or define as bad. I am using these words to describe energy not made from one hundred percent positive/light energy. Light/positive energy is the energy needed to stay healthy.

Your emotions are connected to your health and to your illnesses. They all stem from you and on how positive or negative you are. Remember emotions manifest everything! Emotions will either heal you or make you ill. I believe this is where psychosomatic health and illness is misunderstood. That if we can create psychosomatic illness then we can create psychosomatic health with the understanding of how the Staff of Life works Energetically. By observing and using the Staff of Life to see the affect it has on our physical body, mental/emotional, and spiritual bodies. When we start balancing the negative and positive and putting them back into equilibrium, we will see disease and 'bad' for lack of a better term disappear. This will be interesting to see.

Chapter 30

MANIFESTATION AND THE ELECTROMAGNETIC ENERGY FIELD

To manifest anything you must first start with two components. You need:

(1) Stressors in our lives that create tension or strain within our energy field.

(2) Movement, Motion, or Flow. Emotions are the stressors or tension needed to help you manifest and set into motion the flow to release in the body what is needed to activate your nervous system.

Emotions create the stress or strain between what is happening and what your beliefs or desires are at that moment. Emotions then magnetize the water in your body. To draw to you what you are emotional about. Keep in mind stressors can be either positive or negative. The stronger the emotion the faster it will be drawn to you. There is no discernment. Like energy attracts like energy. The same way a magnet works by drawing the object to it. The stronger the magnet the quicker it will draw the object to it. Remember you MAGNETIZED the water in your body with your emotional response. So you will draw the energy to you just like a magnet does.

When you manifest your negative emotions they create what we call the 'bad' in our lives. Don't blame God. Don't blame the 'Devil', don't blame others. It was all you. You created and made the life you're living. This is the Law of Attraction at work in your life. You have been using it all along. Don't scream it isn't working because it is. It is just not working the way you want it to because you lacked the understanding of what you are doing. You can manifest the good but you need to start getting the knowledge to know how. One way is to stop being negative. By doing this you can manifest more good in your life and less 'bad.' It will not be a yesterday's fix. Keep this in mind. It may take a while but you can do this!

To use it for positive blessings you need to clear out all your negative actions, thoughts, behaviors, rumors, gossiping, etc. Wipe them out! Bring everything into balance. You are manifesting your negative life existence through this Universal Law. All the bad things that have been happening to you is because of your use of the Law of Attraction. Manifesting through your lack of knowledge and understanding on how it really works.

Consciously use the Law of Attraction to magnetize the water in your body with positive energies. Use the positive reactions in your emotions. Then use the Law of Attraction to help change your world and then allow it to reflect out into the world you live in. Really manifest happiness, health, etc. Not just for you but for everyone. But it starts with you! Keep this in mind. You need to heal first and foremost!

Now you need to add Movement or Flow and this comes from your nervous system being kicked into gear with your emotional responses. The chemicals released from your emotional responses affects your nervous system and it creates a flow of energy up your spine. Manifestation has begun. Keep in mind prayer works on the same premise.

Remember everything is a vibration, a frequency, this includes dis-ease as well as your health, happiness and more. Its frequency will ascertain whether you have a good life that is filled with happiness and good fortune or a 'bad' life filled with sadness and ill luck. Your negative or positive actions, thoughts, behaviors, etc. will determine the conditions you create in your life because of your use of the Universal Law of Attraction. Your choice. So stop blaming others for your life, as I have said. You did it. No one else did. If you start taking responsibility for your life you can turn things around. Meaning take responsibility for *all* your actions, thoughts, behaviors, the toxic people you allow in, etc. Do this with complete honesty and courage, not only to yourself but toward others.

Just as others had nothing to do with your life's condition, they will have nothing to do with the turnaround of your life either. It is all you and only you. This information shows you how you did it and will show you how to turn it around. It will not be easy. Sometimes it takes someone from the outside looking in to help you see what you are doing and then change it. You get rid of the negatives in your life by practicing the good in every aspect of yourself.

CHAPTER 31

WE ACT AS TRANSFORMERS AND CAPACITORS

W e need two things to make us attract what we want and don't want in life. They are:

1. Stress=Emotion=Magnetic=Water in our body. Water is a great conductor of electricity. These are connected to the right or God side of your brain. Your unconscious.

2. Flow=Nervous System=Electrical Action=Located in the spinal cord and the nerves in our body and brain. These are connected to the left side or the conscious side of your brain.

These are known in mystical traditions as your Sun and Moon Connections. Is also known as your Solar Conscious or Lunar Conscious. The balancing of these is required to maintain your health in all your spiritual, mental, emotional, and physical aspects.

The electrical part of yourself is similar to the alternating currents of electricity you find in your house and with direct current. The electrical impulses need a path to follow or Flow through. The path is the nerves found in your nervous system. Keep in mind these electrical impulses are always seeking to go to *GROUND*. I am sure you have heard the word ground before. This is the premise behind this word concerning energy in mystical systems of thought.

A release is needed for any excess electrical energy. As I said it needs to go to ground or it will build up and cause you to explode. Triggers release the emotional content. If it is not grounded the only way your body can release the buildup of excess energy is through the emotions, which are connected to your actions. Actions are connected to your nervous system. These are the negative behaviors, actions, thoughts, that we see people exhibiting, especially today. The anger, jealousy, pride, judgments, greed, vengeance, etc., for that matter the seven deadly sins falls into this category too.

So, when you wear rubber soled shoes, you stop the exchange of healing energy that is found in the earth. The rubber soles prevent you from grounding any excess energies. The percentage of energy stored depends on your attitudes, behaviors, thoughts, etc. and how you handle these energies within your energy field and body. If we would walk barefooted more often or learn to ground we could get control of the majority of our negative impulses or explosions. I am not saying this is the only way we release the excess of negative energies but it is a start to understanding the process.

First, we must consider whether or not these energies are more positive or negative in their aspects. You act as a capacitors by storing not only positive/good but negative/bad energies. Seriously, the positive is not an issue unless you have made it a negative. These aspects reflect outward into your environment and life. You need to ask yourself these questions. Are you hanging onto to these emotions? Are you finding ways to release these emotions? Maybe, you are holding them in. Whatever the case may be, they need to be healed or released, especially if you are holding onto negative energies.

If you have stored up a lot of negative emotional energy, you need to find a way to release any excesses of this energy. When you hear people say, *"I can't take it anymore"*, or they say, *"I am ready to explode"*. When these types of statements are being made by someone. They are getting ready to *'short-circuit'*. For example, they explode into violent fits of rage. This is what I am referring to. Their electrical or nervous system is going to short circuit or have a short-out because it is overloaded with negative energies. No different than the electrical system in your house when you overload a circuit. Our nervous system can only hold so much negative energy because we are supposed to be divine by nature. We explode because we are not being spiritually divine. It throws us out of balance. Let's get back into balance.

I also explained that in order to be healthy we need to be more Divine. But the problem is most people become egotistical when they feel they are spirituality more advanced or superior than others. There is nothing wrong with being spiritually more advanced as long as you don't make others feel beneath you, when it comes to their spirituality. You have turned your spirituality and placed it on the side of the negative/bad when you do this. So let us help everyone get higher up in their spiritual advancement.

None of what I have talked about is easy to do. But, if you have chosen the negative then you have lost. Power seduces people whether you are extremely spiritual or extremely bad. We are at half power unless we are totally enlightened. Most chose a path that is more negative or one that is more positive. The choice is yours. But you are only at half power when you choose one or the other. You must be able to control both the negative and positive to be in balance and to be at full power. We need to control the negative aspects of ourselves and not let them control us. When we allow the negative emotions to control us we open the door for others to control and manipulate us.

We also need to be working on our positive side by putting the Divine into everything that we do. We need to guard against imbalances in both aspects of our being because the positive can also be a negative. For example: Love can be out of balance if it turns into an obsession like stalking. Being highly spiritual can turn into a negative if you feel you are spiritually more advanced than others and show it by exhibiting arrogance. This causes people to develop egotistical and condescending behaviors toward others. This is when you know you have been seduced by power. When you have turned the positive Divine energy into something negative. This needs to stop.

Keep in mind POWER SEDUCES and it can affect both the positive and negative aspects of ourselves. *The way to guard against this is to choose right over wrong, or Divine over Bad, or positive over negative.* When you learn this you are well on your way to enlightenment and to manifesting the positive in your life over your negative existence. Be humble!

Our system is also a direct current of electrical energy. How this works is through the characteristic of energy that allows for the transformation of energy. It is the division of this one energy that creates the two alternating currents of energy in our body. This is done through our chakras and energy field.

We take in one energy that we call the Source of All, Creator if you will. When it comes from above through our crown chakra it is at a very high vibration. This vibration, most of us cannot handle if we directly received it. It must travel down through the chakras to lower its vibration for our body to receive this energy and any messages contained within it. This energy however gets transformed with our thoughts, behaviors, actions, etc. into either a positive or negative current. Thus the alternating currents of energy found at the base of the spine is a direct result of this.

We also receive the energy coming up from the earth and it travels through our base chakra. This energy is needed to heal our bodies, another reason not to wear rubber soled shoes. This energy is used to produce healing also. I hope I have given you enough information to help you on your path. I will end here even though there is so much more to say. That will be another book. Blessings to all who read this!

STAFF OF LIFE VARIATIONS

(Figure 1)

DIFFERENT SYMBOLS USED TO EXPLAIN THE SPIRITUAL/ENERGETIC INFORMATION FOR THE STAFF OF LIFE

(Figure 2)

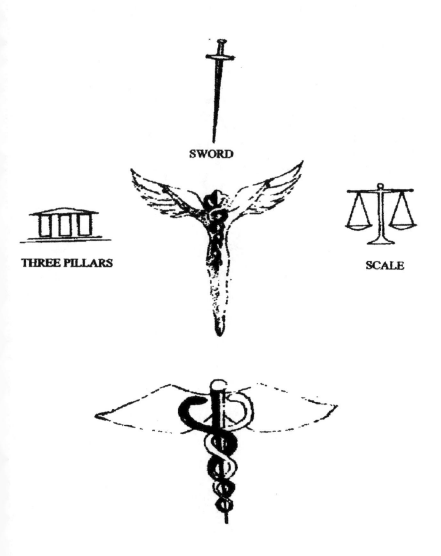

SWORD

THREE PILLARS

SCALE

(Figure 3)

THE WORLDS—LOWER, MIDDLE, AND UPPER WORLDS

RIGHT SIDE OF OUR BRAIN IS REPRESENTED AS THE LOWER OR THE UNDERWORLD. LOCATION OF OUR CONSCIOUSNESS. OUR SEEN WORLD. OUR SEEN WORLD IN WHICH WE LIVE CONSCIOUSLY.

LEFT SIDE OF YOUR BRAIN IS REPRESENTED AS THE THE UPPER OR HIGHER WORLD. THIS IS THE LOCATION OF YOUR UNCONSCIOUS, YOUR GOD SELF. UPPER WORLD. OUR UNSEEN WORLD OR SPIRITUAL WORLD OF ENERGY.

THE BODY IS SEEN AS THE CONNECTION AND MEDIATOR IN REPRESENTING BOTH THE LOWER AND UPPER WORLDS TO INTEGRATE THEM OR NOT THROUGH EGO. ACCESS CAN BE GAINED TO CREATOR BY GETTING RID OF EGO.

OUR BODY, MIND, AND SPIRIT/SOUL HOLDS THESE WORLDS IN EQUILIBRIUM

(Figure 4)

THE ELEMENTS and the CADUCEOUS/STAFF OF LIFE

Wings represent the Element of Air=Breath=Spirit. The mediating element to make things manifest.

Black Serpent represents the Element of Water=Emotion=Magnetism. The imprinting mechanism to manifest what our life is like.

White Serpent represents the Element of Fire=Nervous System=Our Electrical Nature or component of ourselves.

Spinal Column represents the Element of Earth

THE ELEMENTS ARE HELD IN EQUILIBRIUM THROUGH BODY, MIND, AND SPIRIT/SOUL

The Twin Serpents are also known as the symbolic representation of Kundalini Energy. The Yin and Yang. It speaks of the two currents of energy that rest on either side of the central channel in the spinal column that houses our Central Nervous system. They are seen as coiled and dormant until they are awakened and they start an energetic flow of energy up the spine which can sometimes be dangerous if released too quickly. Sometimes the Serpents are described as Dragons.

(Figure 7)

EQUILIBRIUM

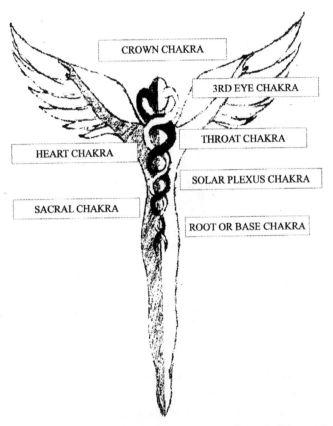

CROWN CHAKRA

3RD EYE CHAKRA

THROAT CHAKRA

HEART CHAKRA

SOLAR PLEXUS CHAKRA

SACRAL CHAKRA

ROOT OR BASE CHAKRA

The chakras are connected to our spinal cord and the Serpent Energy is dormant at the base of the spine. Not totally dormant but we will call it dormant. Both positive and negative currents pass through the chakras as it travels up the spine. Giving each energy center both positive and negative connections. As you can see the serpent energy crosses over at each chakra point along the spine.

For more information:

Contact:

Celeste L Musick
celestelmusick326@yahoo.com
celestelmusick.com

Celeste L. Musick